Welsh Courting Customs

Catrin Stevens

GOMER

First Impression — 1993

ISBN 0 86383 658 5

This book is published with the support of the Welsh Arts Council.

Printed by:
Gomer Press, Llandysul, Dyfed, Wales

CONTENTS

Introduction

For those in love, the period of courtship is an exciting one. It is a time when one feels free of the constraints of childhood and stirred by the onset of puberty. On the other hand, one is not yet ready to take on board the adult responsibilities of 'settling down' to married life.

It can also be a confusing period. This is made more so by its secretive nature, which doubtlessly increases the charm. There seem to be no guidelines, no rule book, to direct the uncertain lover through the infinite maze of emotions and relationships. Yet lovers through the ages have been able to call upon the inherited wisdom, advice and authority of customary practices and rituals to see them through this critical stage of their lives.

This book examines the courtship customs, traditions and beliefs which influenced the Welsh way of life. During the early nineteenth century several English tourists to Wales delighted in such customs as proof of the attractive 'backwardness' of the native population. Yet the search for peculiarly Welsh customs has proved somewhat futile, with the exception perhaps of the celebration of the feast of St Dwynwen, Wales's own patron saint of lovers. The 'rites of passage' of Welsh courtship have in reality much in common with similar rites throughout the peasant societies of Western Europe. The custom of 'courting on the bed', *caru ar y gwely*, for example, was found all along the Western shores of northern Europe, from Scandinavia to Ireland, and was even transported across the Atlantic as 'bundling'. The Welsh *gwerin*, or ordinary folk, clung tenuously to this practice early into the twentieth century, even though it had long since fallen from favour with their more 'sophisticated' English counterparts.

A study of Welsh courtship is necessarily a study of an aspect of Wales's social history. Although it can lead one into the parlour in search of Victorian morals and values, it is much more likely to be concerned with the harsher realities of everyday rural life. Charms and divinations, used to foretell one's future as a lover, appear to be superficial and flimsy material for the serious social historian, but they do, in fact, reflect a deep anxiety, fuelled by economic hardship and social deprivation, which pervaded rural society during this period. No fate could be worse, the young people felt, than to be left 'on the shelf' without a permanent partner in life and with no prospect of entering into the coveted adult world of marriage.

Many of these divinations and fidelity tests popular with young lovers are subtly suggestive of ancient pagan fertility rites. Their powerful influence can be detected lurking beneath and behind some of the most innocent customs and beliefs.

The amusing and apparently harmless practice of fondling girls, to solicit a kiss and a cuddle, on a hayfield appears to be mere rural horseplay, but it can also be viewed as a positive symbol of male dominance, as a fertility rite brutally aggressive in its masculinity. In the same way the crude procedure adopted to pursue a young girl for demeaning her fellow parishioners, by choosing to court a lover from outside her native parish, can hardly be dismissed as just a quaint parochial custom. Often courtship customs offered young people a means of coping with such delicate and ambiguous situations and a study of them can provide us with an insight into the fabric of the society of which they formed an integral part.

One of the most striking aspect of Welsh courtship customs is the degree of continuity over the centuries. Dafydd ap Gwilym, the medieval prince of Welsh love poetry, would have been equally at home amongst the *gwŷr caru* (courting party) of the nineteenth century. He would have known all about going out 'a-knocking' to rouse maidens in the early hours of the morning. He would have greeted them 'under the eaves' with flair before proceeding to find his way, against all odds, into his sweetheart's bed.

This was a continuity deeply rooted in the rural tradition and, thus, it survived in spite of economic crises and social upheavals. It was not until the rural tradition itself was threatened that the old customs gradually lost ground and eventually disappeared.

The Methodist revivalists' zeal against 'popish' superstitions and idle pastimes began the process of erosion in the eighteenth century. Industrialisation and the shift away from rural life which came in its wake further weakened their structure significantly during the nineteenth century. But the final, fatal, blow was dealt by the immense upheaval and questioning of past values in the aftermath of the First Wold War. Traditional Welsh courtship customs could not survive. Those few that did emerge changed as mere shadows of their antecedents, in a much more depersonalized and commercially-minded society.

Acknowledgments

The author wishes to thank the following for their support and help:

The Curator and staff of the Welsh Folk Museum with the research

Bleddyn Davies, who read the transcript and suggested many important changes and corrections

The informants, the length and breadth of Wales, who agreed to be interviewed and quoted

Gomer Press for their encouragement and professionalism.

I
Terry

ABBREVIATIONS

GDG:	Thomas Parry, *Gwaith Dafydd ap Gwilym,* (Cardiff, 1952).
HB:	T H Parry-Williams, *Hen Benillion*, (1956).
O.B.W.V.:	Thomas Parry, (edit.), *The Oxford Book of Welsh Verse*, (Oxford, 1962).
W.F.C.:	Trefor M Owen, *Welsh Folk Customs,* (Cardiff, 1959, Third Edition 1974).
W.F.M.:	Welsh Folk Museum, St Fagans, Cardiff.

Chapter 1

'There's a Crow for Every Crow'

The range and variety of rituals and customs associated with love and courtship illustrate vividly the high importance of the period of courtship in man's life cycle, from birth to death. They were true 'rites of passage', for the period of courtship was never thought of as an end in itself, merely as a means to an end, a means of fulfilling one's ultimate goal of entering into the blessed state of matrimony. Young maidens who dared to defy this convention, by scorning married life, would be gently reminded that 'better a bad husband than no husband at all', a sentiment echoed in a music-hall lyric popular in the late nineteenth century:

> I think we would all prefer
>   marriage with strife
> Than to be on the shelf
>   and nobody's wife.[1]

Consequently, the condition of being left 'on the shelf' was one to be abhorred and avoided if at all possible. *Hen lanciau* (old lads or bachelors), and *hen ferched* (old maids), were often treated with disrespect because it was considered that they had not fulfilled their roles as complete human beings. In Wales this disapproval, 'this clownish ignorance, insensible to the superior duties of celibacy', as Benjamin Heath Malkin described it in 1804, was continued even after death:

> The vulgar and illiberal prejudice against old maids and old bachelors subsists among the Welsh in a very disgraceful degree, so that their graves have not unfrequently been planted by some satirical neighbours not only with rue, but with thistles, nettles, henbane and other noxious weeds.[2]

Since spinsterhood and bachelorhood were considered to be so undesirable, it is hardly surprising that young people expended a great deal of time and energy on trying to foretell the future, on discovering whether they would marry at all and, if so, on predicting who would be the fortunate future partner. Through the centuries a myriad of charms and divinations were evolved to assist the quest for love. It would be tedious, and perhaps almost impossible, to compile an exhaustive collection of all the charms used even in Wales within the confines of this one chapter, so it was decided to concentrate upon the most interesting and representative. Some of the charms have been recorded only in certain areas of Wales and would seem therefore to have a distinctly local flavour. In most cases though, similar beliefs and divinations were found elsewhere. It is undesirable to dogmatize about the specific provenance of most of the charms, for they belong to an international folk culture, as do so many folk-tale themes and folk customs.

Love divinations appear to have developed individually and separately, yet certain elements are common to many of the charms. The figure nine occurs time after time and must have contained strong magical properties in love matters. Many divinations used shoes, stockings and garters, as these, it seems, were common symbols of fertility.[3] In several of the charms, dreams and apparitions were used; and if the hopeful dreamer should see a coffin instead of a future partner, this was always understood to be a death portent. If, on the other hand, the charm failed and nothing appeared in the dream, the enquirer could be sure that he was bound to a fate almost as bad as death itself, never to marry at all. Although, given certain specific conditions, such dreams could occur during any night of the year, they tended to be linked to certain dates. The most important of these were the Three Spirit Nights, *Y Tair Ysbrydnos*, when, according to common belief, supernatural powers were unleashed and the spirits of the dead roamed freely abroad. The three spirit nights were May Eve (30 April), the Eve of St John, or Midsummer's Eve (22 June) and Hallowe'en (31 October) and since this last celebrated the Feasts of All Saints and All Souls and was associated with the commemoration of the dead, it was regarded as the ideal night for trying to work divinations. As individual love charms are described and discussed, these elements and associations will crop up again and again and serve to bind what often appear to be peculiar beliefs and idiosyncratic charms into a cohesive body of folklore.

The popular verse:

> *Gorwedd yn dy wely*
> *A chysga yn dy wâl*
> *Y sawl sy ar dy gyfer*
> *Yr wyt yn siŵr o'i ga'l.*[4]

(Lie in your bed and sleep on your couch. You are sure to get the one that has been destined for you.)

advised aspiring lovers to trust in the hand of fate in matters of the heart rather than put faith in *rhamanta* (romancing) or divinations. Likewise, the old Welsh saying '*Ma brân i bob brân'* (there's a crow for every crow) assured even the most unlikely lover that there was someone destined to be his/her partner. The old maid who added a tail to the saying, '*Mae brân ar gyfer pob brân—pwy ddiawl sy wedi sithu'r 'en frân sy ar yng nghyfer i?'*[5] (There's a crow for every crow—who the devil shot the old crow intended for me?) must have been at her wits' end in her quest for a partner in marriage.

In spite of this advice to leave all to fate, boys and girls were, in fact, introduced to love charms at quite a tender age. School children played the clicking game, pulling their fore-fingers until they clicked, to count the number of their future admirers. Another popular game played during school dinner-time, when plums or prunes were on the menu, was to repeat a counting game which would tell the player firstly what kind of man she would marry and secondly, when the wedding would be. Thus, she could discover whether her future husband would be 'a tinker, tailor, soldier, sailor, rich man, poor man, beggar-man or thief' and whether the wedding would be 'this year, next year, sometime or never'. These sayings could still be heard in school dining-rooms at least within the last twenty years.

'Reading' the leaves in a teacup was one popular way of foretelling the future, though the interpretation could vary from area to area. In Pembrokeshire, if a leaf was seen floating on the surface of the tea this meant that a new suitor was on the horizon. Many leaves indicated many admirers. The size of the leaf would tell whether the prospective lover would be short or tall. A charm could also be worked to foresee when the new lover could be expected. A tea-leaf was placed on the back of one hand and slapped hard with the other. If the leaf was transferred effortlessly to the other hand at the first attempt he would arrive within the week; if the charm worked at the second attempt he would come within a fortnight and so forth.[6] In neighbouring Carmarthenshire a similar charm would be interpreted quite differently. Once again, the floating tea-leaf represented the lover—but one whose love was in doubt. To test his affection, the girl should place a tea-leaf on the back of her left hand and stroke it hard with her right hand. If the leaf became attached to the right hand his love was steadfast, but if it arose at a second or third attempt he should not be trusted and if it did not rise at all, his love was of no value.[7]

Certain old ladies were adept at the craft of reading tea-leaves, as this rhyme suggests:

Dywedodd modryb Catrin
. . . fod Cadi Watcyn
Yn medru dweyd ffortun,
Iddi ddangos yn y cwpan
Wr Nelli Morgan
A'r man gwnai gartrefu,
A nifer ei theulu.[8]

(Aunt Catrin maintained . . . that Cadi Watcyn could tell fortune, That she had shown in the cup Nelly Morgan's husband and where she would make her home and how many children she would have.)

Perhaps Cadi Watcyn used the method of *troi'r ddish*[9] (turning the cup). After drinking the tea the cup containing the 'slop' and tea-leaves was turned around several times and then rested upside down, to allow the leaves to settle. The future could then be 'told' according to the arrangement of the leaves. Naturally, the shape of a heart represented love, but if a row of leaves crossed the heart the affair would end unhappily. The shape of an upside down triangle signified the presence of a third person in the relationship, whilst if there happened to be a star near the heart shape in the cup this meant that the drinker would lead a simple and celibate life.[10]

Young men also consulted love charms to discover their future prospects as lovers, as this example from 1728 indicates:

Let a young man, virgin or widow, note, when they first see a new moon saying at that moment quietly to themselves these words 'Greetings to the moon, Greetings to you, I wish you, moon, to tell me tonight whom my true love will be'. As soon as these words have been spoken they should go to bed and in their first sleep the one they are to marry will appear in a dream.[11]

If a young girl wished to use this charm she could recite it in verse form:

Dacw leuad newydd, rhad Duw arni,
Gyda thi mae'r haul yn codi;
Ac os oes tynged rhyngwy ag un mab
Cyn y bore caf ei weled[12]

(There's the new moon; God bless it. The sun will rise with you. And if any young lad has been fated for me I shall see him before morning.)

For the charm to succeed, the girl should place a pebble in the toe of one of her stockings and put it under her pillow. On the other hand, a Carmarthenshire lass might have chosen a different divination to invoke a dream charm. She could go into the garden, uproot a leek with her teeth and place this under her pillow. One woman testified that this charm had been so successful for her that her lover appeared not in the spirit, but in the flesh and courted in bed with her.[13]

A young girl from the Vale of Ceiriog would not be satisfied with such minor preparations. She would fetch a pullet's egg and mix one half of it with wheatmeal and the other with salt. The two halves would be pressed together and baked in an oven. Once they were ready, the girl ate the salty half and placed the other in the foot of her left stocking under her pillow. After muttering a prayer she would go to sleep, hoping that the spirit of her future husband would appear in her dreams with a glass of water to quench her thirst.[14] This custom was called *teisennau serch* (love cakes) in Anglesey, according to Lewis Morris's cryptic comment:

Teisennau serch, white of an Egg; meal, and salt each; part mix'd into two cakes, eat one and put ye tother under your pillow and you'll dream of your true love.[15]

Variations upon the same theme have been recorded in East Anglia where the charm was particularly associated with St Mark's Eve on 14 April[16] and in Northumberland where the egg would be hard boiled first and the charm linked with the feast of St Agnes:

> Sweet St Agnes, work thy fast,
> If ever I be to marry man,
> Or ever man to marry me,
> I hope him this night to see.[17]

The magical properties of the figure nine enter into several of these dream charms. If there was a newly-wed couple in the area, a young girl could pester them for a piece of their wedding cake. This would be moved nine times back and fore through a wedding ring before being placed under the pillow.[18] In Cardiganshire, nine different species of wood had to be put into a stocking, tied with a tight-legged garter and placed under one's head at night.[19] South Pembrokeshire lasses were also conscientious in their preparations. They had to find the blade bone of a shoulder of mutton and pierce nine holes in it.[20] According to one version of this custom, if the charm were to succeed the girl had to stab the bone repeatedly with a fork at midnight and utter these words:

> 'Tis not this bone I mean to prick,
> But my love's heart I wish to prick
> If he comes not and speaks tonight
> I'll prick and prick till it be light.[21]

Obviously, garters and stockings feature in many of these charms but shoes were also important. A young lad from Radnorshire would tie a garter with nine tight knots and one loose knot and tie this to the bed-post. Next, he would place his shoes in the form of the letter 'T' under his pillow, walk backwards in silence towards the bed,undress with the left hand and repeat this rhyme three times:

> I do this for to see,
> Who my future wife is to be,
> Where she is and what she wears.[22]

This quaint emphasis upon the dream-lover's dress can be found in both the Welsh and English versions of this charm used by young girls.

Dyma'r llythyren 'T'
Gobeithio daw nghariad
I ymweled â fi,
Nid yn lân, nid yn frwnt,
Ond yn ei hen ddillad bob dy'.[23]

(I place my shoes in the shape of a 'T'
Hoping this night my true love to see.
Not in his apparel nor in his array
But in the clothes he wears every day.[24])

The dream charm which involved using an ash leaf was equally complicated. A twig of ash would be sought with five pairs of leaves on each side of a stem and one leaf to the fore. The twig had to be broken off with the left hand. Then the girl would address the leaf, pointing first to the main leaf and say *union onnen* (true ash). She would point in turn to the five pairs of leaves and address them. The first one would be called *dwbwl gangen* (double branch), the second *gwas a morwyn* (best man and bridesmaid), next would come the *clochydd a pherson* (sexton and parson), then the *gŵr a gwraig* (husband and wife) and lastly the two children. She would tie this ash leaf with her left hand and place it next to her bosom. At bedtime, the leaf would be placed by the left hand under the pillow and if all went well, she would be sure to dream of her future husband.[25]

In other versions of this charm the ash leaf was not associated with dreaming, but was used to discover the name of a future lover. Once again, the leaf would be placed next to the heart and the first unmarried person one would meet would bear the same name as the future husband. One young widow was persuaded to test this charm and the first people she met were a nurse carrying a baby boy called Alfred. Her friends laughed when they heard this for there was no-one else called Alfred in the vicinity. Yet, within two years, the widow had met and married the Alfred of her charm.[26] A traditional Welsh verse could be used to facilitate this charm:

Dyma ddeilen bedair dalen
Dynnais i oddi ar y goeden.
Cyntaf un ddaw i'm cyfarfod,
Hwnw fydd fy annwyl briod.[27]

(Here is a four-sided ash leaf I pulled from the tree. The first one who comes to meet me, He shall be my dear husband.)

In East Anglia, on the other hand, it was the lucky clover which worked this charm and it would be placed in the shoe not next to the heart:

A clover or two, a clover or two,
Put it in your right shoe.
The first young man (woman) you meet
In field or street or lane
You'll have him (her) or one of his (her) name.[28]

Other methods could be used to discover the first letter of a sweetheart's name. Perhaps the most unusual and the funniest was recorded by Lewis Morris of Anglesey in the eighteenth century:

3 shell snails from church wall put under a Leeve on a Table nos glangaia (Hallowe'en), will write yr sweethearts name.[29]

The ability of snails to spell was also familiar to the young Caernarfonshire girls:

Byddent hwy yn myned allan
I'r murddunod nos ŵyl Ifan,
Draw i chwilio am falwoden
Wen, i'w rhoddi dan y bowlen.,
Boreu wed'yn bydd y merched
Yno'n darllen coel eu tynged:
Llunio gair o lwybr y falwen,
Os bydd O gwna hyny Owen,
Os yn M gwna hyny Morgan . . .
Ond os erys y falwoden
Yn yr unman dan y bowlen,
Argoel ddrwg yw hyny'n wastad—
Argoel o farwolaeth cariad.[30]

(They would go out to the ruins on St John's Eve to search for a white snail to place under the bowl. The following morning the girls will be reading their fate:forming a word from the snail's path,If it is an O—that will make Owen; if an M—Morgan . . . But if the snail were to stay in the same place under the bowl, That is always a bad omen. A sign of the death of love.)

Apples and turnips could also be used for this purpose, to discover the first letter of a future lover's name. Both turnips and apples had to be peeled carefully in one long narrow strip, for if the peel broke in the peeling the charm could not work. The turnips would be hung behind the kitchen door and the peel buried. The first person of the opposite sex to enter the kitchen would have the same name as the maiden's future husband. This charm was called *bridi-enw* (bride name) in Pembrokeshire.[31] If an apple was used for the divination, the peel would not be buried but tossed over the shoulder and it was thought to fall in the shape of the first letter of the future lover's name. Anne Beale, in her romantic portrayal of the 'Vale of Towey' early in the nineteenth century, used this charm to colour her picture of the merriment at Hallowe'en. A group of friends had gathered to celebrate the feast, to play apple ducking and to foretell the future through peeling apples:

> Rachel threw the apple-paring over her shoulder, and everyone rose to see what shape it would assume. It was an extraordinary hieroglyphic; but some declared it one letter, and some another, the majority deciding in favour of W . . . I cannot permit myself any more such details, but some threw Ns and some As, some Os and others Cs; and some wondered what names X and Z could stand for, and were assured by Polly that those who got such out-of-the-way letters would never marry at all.[32]

A full pea-pod could also be hung behind the kitchen door to await the arrival of a future husband, but it was essential to ensure that the pod contained the magical number of nine peas.[33]

Another charm which emphasized the significance of the number nine was the one popular in Montgomeryshire. On the Eve of All Hallows the young girls would meet to prepare a tasty dish containing nine ingredients including potatoes, carrots, turnips, peas, parsnips, leek, pepper, salt and milk. They would be mashed together into a *stwmp naw rhyw*, (A mash of nine sorts), and a wedding ring added to the concoction. The girl who found the wedding ring in her helping would be the first of the company to marry.[34] Nine girls took part in a similar ritual of making a pancake from nine ingredients in Carmarthenshire, but in this case the ingredients were not divulged and the aim was to eat a ninth portion and then go to bed to dream of the future husband.[35]

As might be expected, some of the charms ventured on Hallowe'en were blood-curdling and demanded courage and determination. Perhaps the most eerie was the custom of walking around the parish church nine times at the approach of midnight. The spirit of the future spouse would appear at the last stroke of twelve to claim his future wife. Ellis Wynne, the famous early eighteenth-century satirist, derided the young girls of his day for believing in this ritual. In his 'Vision of Hell' it was the Devil they saw in the guise of the future bridegroom but the girls were so obsessed by their belief in the charm that they were prepared to marry even the devil himself.[36] To assist in the working of this divination the hopeful lover could choose to carry one of several objects. In Cardiganshire, the young man working the charm would have carried a glove and asked as he went, '*Dyma'r faneg, ble mae'r llaw*?' (Here is the glove, where is the hand?), hoping that his sweetheart would appear to stretch forth her hand and obey his call.[37] Another version from the same area describes the lover carrying a shoe and asking '*Dyma'r esgid, ble mae'r droed*?' (Here is the shoe, where is the foot?) whilst walking, in this case, not around the church but around the dung heap. Such a conscientious lover thoroughly deserved to see his wish fulfilled![38]

One version of this method of divination familiar in the Vale of Glamorgan called for even more daring and attention to detail. At Hallowe'en a large party of young and old gathered together, amongst them 'roistering young fellows' who 'kicked up no little uproar in romping and gambolling with the frisky wenches'. As part of the fun, one of the company was challenged to try 'the trick that should show whom we would marry'. Thus, Ewythr Jenkin was sent to the churchyard by himself and after turning his coat and waistcoat inside out, proceeded to walk around the church. The local expert on charms of this nature, one Catty Evan, had advised him to recite the Lord's Prayer backwards, but he balked at such an act of blasphemy. Having walked around the church 'the right number of times', at his last attempt he entered the porch and placed his finger in the key-hole. Having completed this part of the divination, he returned home, borrowed a pair of garters from one of the girls present, wove them into a true-lover's knot 'saying some fearful words as I plaited them' and laid them under his shirt next to his heart. Before going to sleep, the lover's knot was placed under the pillow and as a result, Ewythr Jenkin dreamt of a beautiful lady.[39] This divination contains several of the elements so associated with love charms, the connection with Hallowe'en, the churchyard, the garters and the dream.

According to Lewis Morris of Anglesey, a similar charm was tried on St John's Eve, being:

> Ye most devilish of all . . . carrying a drawn sword in hand, laying ye scabbard under ye door of ye church and going three times around ye church and pointing the sword towards ye door each time, ye last time your true love or ye Devil will hold ye scabbard for you.[40]

In a modified form of this charm, using a knife instead of a sword, the question would have been '*Dyma'r twca, lle mae'r wain*?' (Here is the knife, where is the sheath?)[41] When these divinations were tried by lads rather than girls it is impossible not to suggest an erotic interpretation.

A similar ritual which was believed to invoke the spirit of a future partner was the rite of sowing hempseed at midnight on one of the Spirit Nights. The future husband or wife was expected to appear in spirit to mow or harvest the crop of hemp. Once again, the sowing was often done in the churchyard and the sower would repeat these words as he/she went, 'Hemp I sow, let him (or her) that comes after me mow'.[42] The Anglesey version emphasizes the possible outcomes of the charm:

> Throwing ye seed over your Head and Looking over your shoulder, and your true love will racke ye ground after you; or a man without a head if ye die before ye years end.[43]

A hopeful enquirer could resort to seeing into the future in a dream if he/she was not brave enough to venture this last charm. He could take the hempseed,

> Throw tenth top over ye head, wrap the rest up in cloth and put it under your pillow, going to bed, without speaking and shall see your true love.[44]

Both Welsh and English versions of the jingles that could accompany the sowing of hempseed have survived. In Tenby, south Pembrokeshire, the girls would go out to crossroads to sow their seeds, for spirits were believed to linger around crossroads. Then at midnight they would chant:

> Hempseed I sow, hempseed I'll mow;
> Whoe'er my true love is to be
> Come rake this hempseed after me.[45]

whilst in Welsh they would urgently call:

> *Y sawl sydd i gydfydio*
> *Doed i gydgribinio.*[46]

(He who would my partner be Let him come and rake with me.)

Carmarthenshire lasses sowed their seeds around the leek bed in the garden.[47] If a young girl should chance to be frightened out of her wits by the vision of her future lover's spirit walking behind her with a scythe over his shoulder to mow the hemp crop, she had only to cry out *Trugarha wrthyf,* (Have mercy upon me), and the apparition would disappear instantly.[48]

In his novel *The Woodlanders*, Thomas Hardy employs this ritual as a pivot on which to swing his plot. The village maidens are described setting out on Midsummer's Eve to sow hempseed while half of the parish follow behind to spy secretly upon them. The sowing continued until midnight, for the girls believed that their future husband would be the first male they would see after twelve o'clock that night. Hardy shows how aspiring admirers would lurk in the shadows ready to spring out in the flesh into the path of their desired lovers. Thus, the heroine, Grace, took part in the ceremony and through mischance or fate, encountered the sophisticated Fitzpiers first after midnight rather than the steadfast, simple, Giles Winterbourne who had loved her so deeply for so long. The consequences of this fateful meeting reverberate through the rest of the novel.[49] Although this is a work of fiction, the use of this divination emphasizes its importance and influence in the nineteenth century. The custom is also mentioned in the work of another Dorsetshire author, in the poem 'Erwin and Linda' by William Barnes and it is easy to sense an erotic undertone to this description. Linda, having sown her seeds, turned to face her future husband:

She saw—and seeing, felt half dead—
A shape came slowly o'er the brook;
And when she saw his scythe-blade's bow
Behind him gleaming by the moon,
She sank with one convulsive throe,
Against an elm-tree in a swoon.[50]

Whether the young people truly believed in the effectiveness of love charms or not, they were certainly prepared to experiment with as many different ones as possible. In Montgomeryshire, they sought to foretell the future by going out on St John's Eve to a nearby well to wash an article of clothing. After washing the garment it would be beaten with a flattened instrument called a bar-staff and the girls would repeat a piece of doggerel similar to the hempseed rhyme, '*Sawl ddaw i gydfydio, doed i gydffatio*' (He who would my partner be, let him come and wash with me).[51] In the Vale of Glamorgan the girls would work this divination in a different way and it was called 'the Maid's trick, which none but true maids were to try'. According to this method, the girl, once the household had retired, would stack the fire and set the table with toasted cheese and other titbits. Then she would strip off her clothes one by one and wash her undergarment, her smock, in a pail of clear spring water. To dry the garment she would lay it over the back of a chair in front of the fire, and then she would retire to bed to dream of her future husband.[52] Ellis Wynne, 'the sleeping bard', associated a similar divination with the Eve of Epiphany and once again brought in the Devil to trick the superstitious maidens who stayed up all night to see who would come to turn the shirts, *troi'r crysau*, they had put out to dry in front of the fire.[53]

One informant could remember hearing of a similar charm being attempted at Tylorstown, in the Rhondda about 1876. Her aunt, who was a pupil teacher, and another young teacher, tried the charm for themselves. They went down to the river nearby and pulled off their shirts. Then they washed the shirts in the water but were careful to ensure that they were pulled through the water against the flow of the river. Once they had finished washing they walked home backwards holding their shirts out before them. At home, the shirts were laid out to dry before the fire and the girls sat down to concentrate in earnest silence upon the forthcoming apparition. Sadly, the young teacher saw a coffin rather than a man's face and indeed, within the year, she had passed away and the prophetic charm had been proved correct.[54]

It was considered unwise to try to interfere in any way with the working of a charm. One farm-girl from Carmarthenshire decided to try the *troi'r crysau* divination, but she had one admirer whom she despised. Her friends decided to play a prank on her and one of the company dressed up in the guise of the hated suitor. When the girl saw this 'poor admirer' walking towards her to claim her as his future wife, she was totally overcome and in spite of all attempts to cajole and console her she died pitifully of a distressed and broken heart.[55]

A similar story has survived of the consequences of interfering with another courtship charm, whereby the hopeful enquirer would throw a ball of wool out of an upstairs window and begin to wind it in, saying '*Myfi sy'n dirwyn, pwy bynnag sy'n dal*' (I am winding, whoever is holding it).[56] The future husband would appear in spirit holding the last piece of wool for the ball. In total innocence, a married couple from Garndolbenmaen, Caernarfonshire, decided to play a trick upon a young maiden who was rather besotted with one of the village lads. The husband disguised himself as the lad and appeared eventually holding the end of the wool. Poor Nan was badly shaken and it was some time before she recovered from the shock.[57]

Before leaving *troi'r crysau* and the other associated charms, it is worth noting a few other miscellaneous divinations which had certain elements in common with those described already. The supper prepared to celebrate May Eve was significant for the maidens of eighteenth-century Anglesey:

Say ye meet on ye Table In ye night. The fair women hideing themselves in ye corners of ye room. Their sweethearts will come in and eat, though a Hundred miles off . . .[58]

while in the 'Vale of Towey', the number of maidens involved in preparing the meal would usually be three:

> In this case the knives, forks and spoons were all placed upside down and everything else turned the wrong way. The girls remained dressed and waited until midnight when a spirit appeared and turned knife, fork and spoon and dish the right way. The apparition of the future partner in this case could be seen only by the girl to whom the man concerned was later to be married.[59]

The maidens of Llanfair Caereinion sought to foretell the future through a visit to the village well at midnight. They would find a frog each and very cruelly they would stick nine pins into each one before reciting a doggerel verse to invoke the apparition of a future lover.[60] Some Carmarthenshire girls used pins also, but in this case they would be stuck into candles and as they burned down to the last and lowest pin the spirits appeared.[61] The candles in the parish church were also frequently used not only to predict the course of courtship but also to foresee who would die during the forthcoming year. To conjure up a vision of a future husband, a girl would light a candle in the church, allow it to burn out completely, leave the church and walk around it three times before walking home to bed in silence.[62]

In passing, it is worth noting a few very localized customs. One was associated with King Arthur's Stone on Cefn Bryn Common on the Gower peninsula. Until the end of the nineteenth century local girls used to place a honey cake soaked in milk upon the stone. Then they would crawl three times on their hands and knees around the stone, hoping that their true lovers would appear in the spirit to join them.[63] Another Gower belief, though not linked with apparitions of a future husband, claimed that the girl who could make a neat sheepskin tray or semmet would be fortunate in her quest for a good husband:

> If you can make a semmet without a crinkle
> You will get a husband without a wrinkle.[64]

As we have seen, many of these divinations, although primarily associated with the three spirit nights, and Hallowe'en in particular, could also be successfully attempted on other nights of the year. However, the love charms using nuts, wheat grains and ivy leaves do seem to have been particularly linked to the celebrations at Hallowe'en, when parties would be held to prepare for the beginning of the dark winter season. Nuts and wheat grains, with their hard outer shells which could be popped to reveal a soft kernel, symbolized the hope that life could suddenly explode anew even at this very dark time of the year. Thus, in the north of England, Hallowe'en would sometimes be called Nut-cracking Night and it was considered that if a nut thrown into a fire on this evening would 'pop' the thrower could hope for a happy love life:

> If you love me pop and fly,
> If not there silently lie.[65]

In the Llandysul area, a brightly burning nut indicated marriage within the year.[66] Wheat grains were also placed in the fire to help predict the future. A boy and girl would place a wheat grain each on a shovel and this would be heated on the fire. Presently, the grains would edge towards one another, gradually swelling and eventually popping from the shovel into the fire. If both grains shot off at the same time the young couple would jump into marriage together, but if they popped off at different times, or in different directions, the course of their love would not be smooth.[67]

A similar charm could be worked with ivy leaves, though Lewis Morris's passing reference to '*dail eiddew mewn dŵr nos glangaiaf*' (ivy leaves in water at Hallowe'en), does not explain the Anglesey version of this custom.[68] In Cardiganshire, however, the leaves would be thrown into the fire, not into water, to predict the course of one's future love life. Both pointed male leaves and rounded female leaves were gathered and thrown into the fire. Should the male and female leaves jump, as they heated, towards one another, this indicated a successful courtship; should they jump away from one another the lovers would never marry. It is easy to imagine the impact such predictions could have during the merrymaking and horseplay of a Hallowe'en party.[69] The ashes from the fire could also be used to foretell the future, as in this complex explanation from Cardiganshire:

> Three furrows were made in the ashes which had fallen from the fire; the person who wished to find out whom she would marry was to think of the names of three young men, one of which she gave each furrow. Another person asks her three questions: 1. Whom will you love? 2. Whom will you marry? 3. Who will throw you over the bed? As each question is asked, the questioner points to one of the three furrows in turn beginning with any one of them. The set of questions is then repeated, six times in all, in the following order: 123, 321, 231, 213, 312, 132. Whichever furrow is last but one touched is the person she is to have.[70]

Another method of divination popular in the Llandysul area on the Eve of All Hallows, was to place three bowls on a table, the first containing clean water, the second dirty or troubled water and the third filled with soil. The person who wished to know his destiny as a lover would be blindfolded and led towards the table. If he should place his hand in the bowl of soil he would be fated to die without marrying; if in the dirty bowl his married life would be full of strife and trouble; while the clear, clean water was taken as a sign of a happy marriage.[71] Marie Trevelyan, however, offers different interpretations for the charm of the three bowls, for, according to her sources, clean water predicted widowhood, dirty water married life and an empty bowl spinster or bachelorhood.[72]

Although the use of such charms and divinations, based as they were on superstition, must have been pagan in origin, we have already noted how many of them had become associated with the churchyard and even the church. It is not surprising, therefore, that the Bible could also play a role in predicting the future. The usual method would be to turn to the Book of Ruth in the Old Testament and to read aloud the verses expressing Ruth's undying love for her mother-in-law, Naomi:

> And Ruth said, Intreat me not to leave thee, or to return from following after thee:for whither thou goest, I will go; and where thou lodgest, I will lodge:thy people shall be my people, and thy God my God.
>
> Where thou diest, I will die, and there I will be buried:the LORD do so to me, and more also, if ought but death part thee and me. (Ruth 1:16-17)

The young lad taking part in the romancing would present his sweetheart with a large front-door key which would be laid to rest upon these verses. The Bible would be closed and tied securely with a piece of string. Then the girl would balance the key on her left-hand ring finger and this, in turn, would rest upon the boy's right-hand index finger. Having completed such complicated preparations, the boy would ask the girl, '*Ai ti sydd i fod yn wraig imi*?' (Are you to be my wife?) and if this was so, the Bible would spin of its own accord towards the girl. The charm would be reversed, and the girl would ask the boy the appropriate question.[73]

The English version of the Bible charm was not between two lovers but was used to reveal the first letter of a future lover's name. As one enquirer supported the key and the book an assistant would ask 'If . . . be the letter of my true lover's name, may the Bible turn round and the key do the same' and the Bible would eventually turn or fall at the relevant letter.[74] Verses from the Song of Solomon (Chapter 8:6-7), 'Love is strong as death, jealousy is cruel as the grave' could also be used for these charms as an alternative to those from the Book of Ruth.[75]

Many of the methods of romancing described above were still practised in Wales within living memory. Consequently it proved possible to interview informants and gather oral testimony about such divinations, testimony which showed that they were a living and vibrant part of the traditional folk culture. The informants not only consulted the charms, but also believed quite sincerely that they worked and that their predictions were true. They could cite examples and describe the consequences. Yet most of these quaint and attractive customs have died out by today. The Bible charm which was furtively consulted in Cardiganshire in the mid 1950s has disappeared, and the celebrations associated with Hallowe'en have been thoroughly commercialized and Americanized. Yet though the old methods have fallen into disrepute and disuse, young people still try to discover what their prospects will be as lovers and as marriage partners. They seek the aid of age-old astrologers who can now plot the future with elaborate charts based on computer data and futuristic technology. It seems that man and woman's curiosity to find out about his/her destiny in the field of love and courtship will never be eliminated but will continue to fascinate, albeit in a much altered way, young lovers for generations to come.

NOTES

[1]John R Gillis, *For Better for Worse, British Marriages, 1600 to the Present* (Oxford, 1985), (Gillis), pp.233-4.

[2]Benjamin Heath Malkin, *The Scenery, Antiquities and Biography of South Wales* (London, 1804, re-printed 1970), p.608.

[3]A H Krappe, *The Science of Folklore* (London, 1930), p.279.

[4]W.F.M. Mss 3472/2 Mary Jones, Pennant, Dyfed.

[5]Oral testimony, Kate Davies, Pren-gwyn, Llandysul, Dyfed.

[6]Rev W Meredith Morris, *A Glossary of the Demetian Dialect of North Pembrokeshire* (Tonypandy, 1910), p.54.

[7]Parch D G Williams, Ferndale, 'Casgliad o Len-gwerin Sir Gaerfyrddin', *Cofnodion a Chyfansoddiadau Buddugol Eisteddfod Llanelli, 1895,* edit. E Vincent Evans (1898), p.342.

[8]*Cerddi Cymru,* Hen a Diweddar, Cyfres III (Bala), pp.4-6.

[9]Morris, p. 310.

[10]Eirlys Gruffydd, 'Rhamantu a Dail te', *Llafar Gwlad,* vol.5.

[11]John Jones, (Myrddin Fardd), *Llén Gwerin Sir Gaernarfon,* (Caernarfon, 1909), pp.147-8.

[12]Bangor Mss 1589 (1908), p.75.

[13]Williams, p.358.

[14]Rev W Rhys Jones, (Gwenith Gwyn), W. F. M. Mss 2593, 'Llen Gwerin Dyffryn Ceiriog', p.89.

[15]Hugh Owen, *The Life and Works of Lewis Morris (1701-1765),* (1951), p.144.

[16]Enid Porter, *The Folklore of East Anglia* (London, 1974), p.23.

[17]M Baker, *Discovering the Folklore and Customs of Love and Marriage* (1974), p.10.

[18]Williams, p.352.

[19]*Bye-gones*, 29 Sept., 1897.

[20]*Tales and Traditions of Tenby* (1858), p.29.

[21]Edward Laws, *The History of Little England beyond Wales* (London, 1888), p.409.

[22]*Bye-gones,* 15 July, 1896.

[23]Williams, p.353.

[24]Oral Testimony, Mrs R Stevens, East Coker, Yeovil, formerly of Pontypool, Gwent. See also, Baker, p.7 and Porter, p.23.

[25]W.F.M. Mss 3472/2.

[26]*Cymru Fu,* 23 July 1881, p.7.

[27]*Bye-gones,* 24 Jan., 1894; T H Parry-Williams, *Hen Benillion, (HB)* (1956), 353.

[28]Porter, p.23.

[29]Hugh Owen, p.143.

[30]John Jones, (Myrddin Fardd), p.135.

[31]Morris, p.40.

[32]Anne Beale, *Traits and Stories of the Welsh Peasantry* (London, 1849), pp.86-7.

[33]*Bye-gones*, 5 Aug., 1891.

[34]T G Jones, 'A History of the Parish of Llansantffraid-ym-Mechain', *Montgomeryshire Collections*, vol. iv, 1871, p.140.

[35]Williams, p.354.

[36]Ellis Wynne, *Gweledigaethau y Bardd Cwsc,* introd. by Aneurin Lewis, (Cardiff, 1960), p.132.

[37]S R Meyrick, *History and Antiquities of Cardiganshire* (1810), p.56.

[38]David W Harries, 'Tests of True Love', *Country Quest,* June, 1974, pp.35-6.

[39]Charles Redwood, *The Vale of Glamorgan, Scenes and Tales among the Welsh,* (London, 1839), pp.5-12.

[40]Hugh Owen, p.144.

[41]*Bye-gones,* 25 June, 1873; Wirt Sikes, *British Goblins* (London, 1880), p.305.

[42]Peter Roberts, *Cambrian Popular Antiquities* (1815), p.130.

[43]Hugh Owen, p.144.

[44]Ibid., p.143.

[45]*Tales and Traditions of Tenby,* pp.27-8.

[46]Sikes, p.304.

[47]*Bye-gones,* 29 Sept., 1897.

[48]John Jones, (Myrddin Fardd), p.154.

[49]Thomas Hardy, *The Woodlanders* (London, 1974), pp. 174-180, 397.

[50]Baker, p.6.

[51]*Bye-gones,* 25 June, 1873.

[52]Redwood, pp. 16-21.

[53]Ellis Wynne, p.132.

[54]Oral testimony. Glenys Thomas, Awelon, 2 Waun Lon, Porthcawl, 28 Dec., 1983.

[55]Williams, p.354.

[56]John Jones, (Myrddin Fardd), p.153.

[57]Oral testimony, Mrs Sian Jones, Tŷ Penfro, Bryncir, Garndolbenmaen, 2 Jan 1984.

[58]Hugh Owen, p.144.

[59.] Beale, pp.89-92.

[60]T Gwynn Jones, *Welsh Folklore and Folk Custom* (London, 1930), p.114.

[61]Williams, p.354.

[62]*Cambrian Journal,* 1860, pp. 68-70.

[63]Sian Llewellyn, *Customs and Cooking from Wales* (Swansea, 1974), p.22.

[64]I C Peate, *Guide to the Collection of Welsh Bygones* (1929), p.44.

[65]Beale, pp.84-5; Baker, p.8. A Porteous, *Forest Folklore* (London, 1928), p.266.

[66]W J Davies, *Hanes Plwyf Llandyssul* (Llandyssul, 1896), p.253.

[67]Redwood, p.3.

[68]Hugh Owen, p.144.

[69]Meyrick, p.56.

[70]Ibid., pp. 56-7.

[71]W J Davies, p.253.

[72]Marie Trevelyan, *Folk-Lore and Folk-Stories of Wales* (London, 1909), p.238.

[73]John Jones, (Myrddin Fardd), pp. 149-150.

[74]Oral Testimony, Mrs R Stevens, East Coker, Yeovil, formerly of Pontypool, Gwent.

[75]Edwin Grey, *Cottage Life in a Hertfordshire Village* (1924), p.152.

Chapter 2

'Swaggering and Foxing'

The daily and monthly round of agricultural work accorded farm-servants very little time for recreation and leisure. Divinations and romancing did allow young lovers to communicate through dreams and apparitions, but realizing and fulfilling the relationships promised in those charms often proved to be a much more tantalizing proposition.

Stockmen on the Llŷn Peninsula during the last century worked from five in the morning until eight at night, 'practically from the time men get up 'till the time they have supper and go to bed', while a waggoner's day at Llangamarch, Powys would run thus, 'Bait the horses at 6am, out work with team at 6.30; in at 11 till 2pm; out again till 6pm, finish for the night at 8pm'.[1] The working day would end with supper; a basin of broth or milk, bread and cheese. The maid-servants would work even longer hours for they would be the earliest to rise in the morning and the latest to retire at night. Indeed the old adage:

> Man's work is from sun to sun
> But a woman's work is never done.

was aptly quoted in the 1893 *Commission on Labour, The Agricultural Labourer.*[2] During the weekends the regime would be less rigorously maintained as farm-servants generally finished work at 4pm on Saturdays and on Sundays the men would only be expected to tend the livestock while the girls prepared the meals.

It would seem logical, in the face of such a rigid routine, that at the weekends the young people would grasp at every possible opportunity to meet, mix and form experimental relationships. There were, however, subtle constraints upon such freedom of movement. Maid-servants usually 'lived in' and were therefore always available for work. They also came under the direct and vigilant supervision of the mistress in the farmhouse who assumed parental responsibility for the moral welfare of her charges. Thus, rather incongruously, general gallivanting and casual flirtations were severely frowned upon, while, as will be seen later, more serious personal relationships within the farmhouse itself were delicately tolerated and even secretly encouraged. On a day-to-day basis, any public display of mutual affection between two young people was condemned and anyone found 'guilty' of such an indiscretion 'would be considered impolite, impudent and disreputable'. They could expect 'to be denounced by the unanimous voice of society'.[3]

Yet society realized full well that young people could not possibly be expected to accept such exacting strictures indefinitely. Safety valves had to be provided, and these came in the form of the annual calendar of feasts and festivals which were dotted throughout the agricultural year. The rites and customs associated with these festivals provided organized recreation, especially before 1850 when the nonconformist bodies began to develop their own very sober leisure activities such as literary meetings, concerts and *eisteddfodau*. Without doubt the most important of these festivals for the farm-servant populace were the annual and semi-annual hiring fairs.

The traditional fairs of Wales were vital as economic institutions in a country with few large market towns. They were also important as meeting places for the local people, and especially for the youth of the area. This was obviously an age-old custom, for Bedo Brwynllys, a medieval poet, mentions how he first glimpsed his true love at a fair.[4] The hiring fairs might be held twice yearly on specific dates in April/May and September/October/November, though the autumn ones were generally the most popular. Servants would travel from fair to fair, not only to seek the best place of employment, but also to acquaint themselves with the 'sweetheart talent' of the area. Llangyfelach Fair in Glamorgan, held on the very early date of St David's Day, 1 March, must have been one of most popular, for it attracted followers both from the agricultural lands to the north and west, and from the industrial towns of the south and east. 'People flocked there in their thousands, some came in carriages, others on horseback, and on foot; they came in crowds upon crowds. And on arriving at the Llan fair one would find there young girls and boys from Monmouthshire, Glamorganshire, Carmarthenshire, Cardiganshire, Pembrokeshire, Breconshire and Radnorshire.'[5]

Hiring Fair: a stylized picture of a ninenteenth-century hiring fair
(National Library of Wales)

The girls came to the fairs in their best finery:

Morynion fydd mor grandied i'w gweled yno i gyd,
Pob un mor hardd a'i meistres gerbron ar hyn o bryd,
A'u shawls a'u gownau sidan a'i bonnets 'kiss me quick',
Rhubanau, artificials, i hudo Deio a Dic.[6]

(Maids so grand will all be there to see,Each one as beautiful as her mistress before us now, With their shawls and silk gowns and 'kiss me quick' bonnets, Ribbons, artificials (false flowers worn ornamentally) to charm Deio and Dick.)

Their main aim, as the following extract from a Cardiganshire ballad illustrates, was to secure a lover on fair day:

Mae'n dda gan y march gael pedolau,
Mae'n dda gan yr ychen gael gwair;
Mae'n dda gan y merched bach ifainc
Gael cariad ddod adre o ffair.[7]

(The stallion likes to have horseshoes, The oxen like to have hay,The young lasses like to have a sweetheart to come home from a fair.)

It is hardly surprising that young men, who had given up work as farm-servants in order to migrate to the industrial south, should try to return to their home areas to enjoy the fun of the autumnal hiring fairs. One girlfriend chastised her sweetheart for not promising to return to accompany her to the fair for he would be 'making small of her and that she was going to look for another one against the fair'.[8] In West Pembrokeshire, the young servants would proceed from St David's fair on the first Tuesday of October, to Portfield Fair, Haverfordwest, on the fifth, Fishguard on the eighth, Mathri on the tenth and thence to the 'runaway fair' at Letterston on the third Monday of the month. This fair was so-called as it gave those who had 'run away' from their new place of service after only a few days' trial an opportunity to re-engage themselves to other employers.

As part of the hiring procedure, which would be the main business of the early morning at the fair, the farm-servant received a pledge of a shilling, *ern*, to seal the contract of employment. This money would prove to be very useful during the following hours as the young men wandered among the stalls or *standins*, looking for *ffeirin* (fairing), to buy for their favoured girlfriends. They might choose an apple, a cake, a handkerchief or some nuts as their fairing, while at Llanarth fair in Cardiganshire, a boy would treat his girlfriend to a bowl of soup for a halfpenny.[9] China fairings, especially those depicting lovers on a bed, and called bed pieces, were very popular in late Victorian times. Made in Germany, mostly *c.*1860-1890 they often carried suggestive inscriptions such as 'Shall we sleep first, or how?' Such generosity did not bind the receiver to the giver for the fair day, however, and most girls would hope to return home laden with many fairings received from several different sweethearts. A country poet, Ben Evans of Dan-garn, Mynachlog-ddu (Pembrokeshire) at about the beginning of this century, felt particularly aggrieved that he should have wasted his fairing on a fickle sweetheart. At Maenclochog fair he met a girl from nearby Llan-y-cefn:

. . . Gofyn imi wnaeth am ffeirin,
Prynes iddi chwech sgadenin.

Rown i'n meddwl bod yn hapus
Gyda merch fach lan ddifyrrus;
Ond fe gefais wir fy mhoeni—
'Roedd un arall am ei charu . . .

Ond o'r diwedd bu'n rhaid ildio,
Bachgen arall oedd hi'n leicio;
Wedi i fi hala'r arian
Bachgen arall fwyto'r sgadan![10]

(She asked me for a fairing, I bought her six herrings. I intended to have a good time With an attractive, pleasant young girl; But I was indeed cursed—Another one wanted to court her . . . But at last I had to yield, It was the other lad she fancied; After I had spent the money It was the other lad who ate the herrings!)

A china fairing called a bed piece, depicting, appropriately, courting on the bed. It was probably made in Germany c. 1860-1890.
(by kind permission of Dr Dilys Quick)

Likewise, another Pembrokeshire rhymester showered his new sweetheart with expensive fairings at Mathri fair:

Pheeby was a buwty girl
  I meet in Mathry fare—
Cheecs like apples eis like a star
  No better wan was there.

An Pheeby tak me ole about
  The standins an the shows
An I was tret her ole the day—
  She mak the munny goes.

I gave har jugs an jingerbread
  An blankt an a cwilt,
An wen the rain was ouful bad
  We have a drop in tilt.[11]

His generosity proved to be of no avail as she chose another to escort her home!

As they walked amongst the stalls the boys and girls would form into small groups. These groups would eye one another and exchange flirtatious remarks. This custom is vividly described by one Pelagius in the Baptist publication *Seren Gomer* in 1828. He utterly deplored the way young women came together:

> to parade about, half a dozen of them, arm in arm; heedless of their appearance, mocking in the midst of the fire of tribulation . . . Talking across the street, laughing like idiots, and with their flirtatious eyes darting to and fro, . . . They are not seen making purchases as that is not their message, rather do they stroll about haughtily and shamelessly, all virgin modesty forgotten . . . and feminine beauty totally abolished.

The boys behaved in a similarly robust and rude manner and when two opposite groups did chance to meet, the boys would surround the girls and pen them in the middle, 'they (the boys) place their arms over the napes of their necks, drag them by their hands and break out into laughable and barbaric comments'.[12] In the Bala area this custom was called *yswagro pen ffair* (swaggering at the fair), and the youths used to flock to the Bala May Day fair specifically to 'swagger about'. The 'swaggering' would begin at about one o'clock and by four or five o'clock the groups would have dissolved into couples.[13] When two groups of local lads chanced to meet as they were 'swaggering' the outcome would be a contest for the girls, as in the folksong from Penmorfa, Caernarfonshire, which reads in translation:

> The lads of Na(n)mor with their sweethearts
> Were a-swaggering at Penmorfa fair,
> Tra la lemdo, tra la lemdo!
>
> But Fron's farm-servant and 'Nysfor's husbandsman
> Took them away from the Na(n)mor boys.
> Tra la lemdo, tra la lemdo.[14]

Another convention might be used to attract the attention of a prospective girlfriend. The aspiring lover would send a *llatai*, a messenger or intermediary on his behalf *i hala i moyn* (to go to fetch) the girl. The boy would ask his friend, '*Cer i moyn hon a hon i fi'* (Go to fetch so and so for me) even though she might be within earshot. The intermediary would then approach the girl and say 'so and so is asking whether you will come' and after some flirting and persuasive talk she would probably agree.[15] A popular and attractive girl would expect to be 'fetched' from several different directions on fair day, a custom called *mofyn a thynnu* (fetching and drawing), in Cardiganshire and Carmarthenshire, as in this description from the parishes of Llangeler and Pen-boyr:

> Once the young girl had sat down with some chosen youth, someone else would 'send to fetch' her and 'draw' her in an attractive way to him. Then she would be 'fetched' back again or someone else might draw her, and thus on the girl would go from one lover to a new one, receiving cakes from each one to place in her handkerchief, until it was time to go home.[16]

This custom was known as *erlid merch* (chasing a girl) in the Vale of Glamorgan and it was said that there were *dau fachan yn powlo* (two boys (?) bowling/competing) for a popular girl.[17] This situation also led to arguments and even fighting:

> Let us say that Mari Cwmgeist (name of a farm) is going to Llandysul fair, and since she is a pretty little wench, Sam Gwarcoed

> might fancy courting her. This is how he would proceed:He would send Wil Molhedog to her, to fetch her to the tavern to receive a fairing. If she went with him, and if there was a great deal of fetching for her, very soon, Sam Penrallt would come to fetch her for Ifan Glanclettwr; and there would be a heated argument about her. Sometimes the lads would fight quite fiercely for a girl. Now the best man in her opinion would be the one chosen to escort her home.[18]

Several of these descriptions show that the 'swaggering' and flirting eventually led the young couples into the beer 'tilts' or tents, the smuggling pubs opened especially for fair days, or into the taverns to *yfed ati* (drink away). Once again Pelagius, through his stringent criticism of the custom, provides a graphic picture of the carousing which resulted:

> In a tavern on a fair day, one finds the young people higgledy-piggledy, pulling and pushing, and dragging one another over chairs, tables, beds; spilling beer . . . And here they will remain until the dark of night, and later, sometimes singing, sometimes quarrelling, and often the companionship will end in a fight.

The girls played an active role in the boisterousness for they would protect their sweethearts, take part in their battles, and ensure that no one stole them away from them.[19]

Many of the other nineteenth-century denominational publications supported these views and denounced the custom of *yfed ati*. As one such propagandist pamphlet claimed:

> One of the most odious customs of the fair is the dragging of young girls into taverns . . . There they sit in the middle of the slime, the noise and the riotous behaviour of a group of drunkards in the tavern, listening to their cussing and swearing. The outlook for a girl who can sit and enjoy such companionship can only be bleak. The 'fair night' has proved to be a dark, black and destructive night for many a pure and virtuous maiden . . . They are forced under a cloud of shame and disgust to remember the fair night as the night of their fall.[20]

This custom was called *cwmnïa* (keeping company) in the Aman Valley, Carmarthenshire and it was denounced by one ardent temperance supporter for inciting young people to 'drink together, excite each other . . . to go home together and in the end to fall into the same ditch of prostitution together'.[21]

When the young couples eventually tired of the bawdy companionship of the taverns they would begin to wander homewards. The night would still be young and they would be 'foot loose and fancy free' as flighty Polly Garter so jauntily observed in *Under Milk Wood*:

> Now when farmers' boys on the first fair day
> Come down from the hills to drink and be gay,
> Before the sun sinks I'll be there in their arms
> For they're good bad boys from the lonely farms.[22]

The farm-servants would have changed employers during the fair day and they would, by the evening, be free of their old masters, yet not under the direct supervision of their new employers. The *Commission on Labour, The Agricultural Labourer* in 1893 explains the consequences of such unaccustomed freedom:

> There is no fixed rule as to where the liberated servants are to go to sleep on the fair nights. Sometimes they go to their parents' home; sometimes to the farm which they left in the morning. The girls, if so inclined, may mislead their parents by suggesting they intend returning to the farm, whilst they may also mislead their mistresses by intimating their intention of going home. The result is that there have been cases where girls have by this device been able to stay late in the town, but have then become afraid of going into the farm dwelling-house, and have been induced to spend the night in the outbuildings instead. Shame and disgrace are the almost inevitable consequences.

The Commissioner linked this tendency with the very high rate of illegitimacy in the rural areas of Wales; an annual average for the five years from 1884 to 1888, of 114 per 1,000 births.[23] Recent research on popular recreation in rural England during the first half of the nineteenth century seems to corroborate this evidence. Statistics from Bromley in Kent show that there was a significant bulge of illegitimate births in December—January, about nine months after the spring fair and the popular ballad on the 'Wrekington Hiring' emphasizes this link:

> . . . they danc't agyen till it was day,
> An' then went hyem, but on the way,
> There was some had rare fun they say,
> An' found it nine months after—O . . .[24]

This was also the impression gained by E. Tegla Davies when he came to Menai Bridge, Anglesey, as a young minister towards the beginning of the twentieth century. In his autobiography he describes how he had endeavoured to end the chapel meeting at Llanfair Pwllgwyngyll promptly at seven in order to return at once to Menai Bridge to enjoy some of the merriment of the annual and infamous *Ffair y Borth*. But he was devastated by what he saw:

> 'As I returned I noticed . . . clusters scattered here and there on hedges by the side of the road, every now and then . . . on looking more carefully I was dismayed . . . to see that they were young lads and lasses in sexual intercourse, quite openly, and not trying to hide themselves even when the lamp light fell on them.'

In his distress Tegla turned to a doctor friend for advice but he merely smiled and said 'Yes . . . this is the day for populating the county. There will be plenty of work for doctors, if they are needed, within nine months.'[25]

These descriptions tend to highlight the darker side of courting at hiring fairs. Not all the participants fell upon such wanton ways and many could look back upon the 'fetching and drawing', the 'swaggering' and 'drinking away' with affection, amusement and even gratitude. The hiring fairs did allow young farm-servants to meet and mix together without inhibition and helped to dissolve normal restraints and sanction what would on other occasions be less acceptable. They played a vitally constructive role in the social pattern of rural nineteenth-century Wales.

The hiring fairs heralded the beginning of the dark, winter season, and what few opportunities presented themselves for social intercourse during this period were seized upon and exploited with alacrity. *Nosweithiau Llawen* (merry evenings) and *Cymorth* (benefit) nights were often organized and attended by young people.[26] Young women would give a day's work, spinning or knitting to help a poor person and the young men would join them towards the end of the evening. Love tokens would be given:

> These pledges were handed to the respective lasses by the different Caisars and Merry Andrews'—persons dressed in disguise

for the occasion, who in their turn, used to take each his young woman by the hand to the adjoining department, where he would deliver the pwysi or nose-gay, as it was so called, and immediately retire upon having mentioned the giver's name.[27]

Likewise the *cwrw bach*, (small beer), another benefit event, encouraged drinking, carousing and courting. At an Amanford *cwrw bach* the lads would toss dice to win *pice*, (Welshcakes), and these would be divided between the girls. The girl with the most *pice* in her apron at the end of the evening was considered to be the most desirable sweetheart.[28] A Breconshire biographer criticized the *cwrw bach* as a 'breeding place of immorality and licentiousness' and this aspect was borne out by a newspaper report of a paternity suit in 1859 which claimed that the young girl had fallen under the charms of a butcher from Burry Port, Carmarthenshire during such an evening.[29]

Pilnosau (peeling evenings) for preparing rushes for rushlights, *nosweithiau pluo* (feathering evenings) preparing the poultry for the Christmas season, and *nosweithiau gwneud cyflaith* (toffee-making evenings) would also be transformed into social gatherings. Hugh Evans in his minor classic *The Gorse Glen*, which recalls rural Denbighshire in the late nineteenth century, describes the atmosphere at a *noswaith weu* (knitting evening):

> The guests were usually young people, both male and female. The girls arrived first, and it was considered to be the proper thing for the young men to linger a little before putting in an appearance . . . The *noswaith weu* was a great clearing house for local gossip and for rumours of courtship. Sometimes the invitations would be so arranged that a couple who were suspected to be courting would be invited, and the reactions when they met or talked to each other would be watched by keen and interested eyes.[30]

The Christmas period, the *gwyliau* (holy days) provided several opportunities for socializing. *Gwaseila* (wassailing), was originally a pagan fertility rite and when the party of male wassailers had arrived at a house and eventually gained entry through song there would be a feast of entertainment. The young men would choose their hosts with care, not only for their generosity, but also for the female company present, as this reference in a popular wassailing song suggests:

Hyd yma ni ddaethon oherwydd ni glywson
Fod merched glan, tirion yn tario yn eich llys . . . [31]

(We have come this far because we have heard that there are pure, sweet maidens staying in your court.)

On New Year's Eve it was customary in Carmarthenshire and Pembrokeshire to hang a *llwyn cusanu* (a kissing bush) of holly, decorated with ribbons and fruit in every home. The menservants would try to catch the young maidens under the evergreen bush but before they could kiss, the boy would have to present the girl with a pair of gloves. One informant noted that his grandmother had never bought herself a new pair of gloves until she was almost seventy years old. [32]

During the same festive period the custom of 'hunting the wren' would bring young people together. According to Edward Lhuyd, the seventeenth-century antiquary and scholar, 'They are accustomed in Pembrokeshire etc. to carry a wren in a bier on Twelfth Night; from a young man to his sweetheart, that is, two or three bear it in a bier with ribbons, and they sing carols'. [33] No other source on this custom mentions the romantic significance of the wren but, rather unexpectedly, there is a much later reference to young girls joining in the hunting itself as members of the carol-singing party. This was one of the verses sung by the party which sought admittance to the house:

Mae yma i chwi'ch dewis o ferched hoenus iach,
'Tifeddesi tirion tawel a breiniol uchel ach,
Cewch gofleidio a chusanu nes bo ar frig y dydd.
A myn'd â hi i'r gwely os yn boddloni fydd. [34]

(You have here a choice of healthy, lively girls, Gentle and quiet heiresses and of a high and honourable degree, You may cuddle and kiss until the break of day And take her to bed if she agrees (or if she pleases you).)

During the following winter months there would only be the occasional *noson weu, pilnos,* or even funeral wake to enliven the social scene. It is hardly surprising that the celebration of St Valentine's Day, on 14 February, should have gained such a following and this festival will be examined in full in a later chapter.[35] Then came the solemnity of Lent and, although self-denial and penance were not over-emphasized by nonconformists, yet it was not a seemly time for lively merrymaking. With the coming of Easter, the Feast of Resurrection, the interrupted pleasures of life could be resumed, this time in the pleasant setting of spring. On Easter Monday and Tuesday the 'lower orders' engaged in the custom of 'lifting' or 'heaving' whereby a party of lifters, men on Monday and women on Tuesday, would roam the neighbourhood looking for members of the opposite sex to 'lift', or 'heave' in their chairs. Once the victim had been lifted into the air three times he or she would be kissed and in return the lifters would receive a small gift or 'reward' for the favour. Various interpretations[36] have been put forward to explain the origin of this ritual, linking it with the commemoration and re-enactment of the Resurrection. But by the last century the custom was little more than a jolly social event. The young men would seek out favoured girlfriends 'to lift', although older women would also go through the same ordeal. By 1880, much of the original spontaneity had evaporated and, in Cheshire, one William Pullen brought charges against some local youths who had entered his house 'to lift' his wife. Although the youths argued that they were merely 'endeavouring to carry out an old Cheshire custom', this did not impress the magistrates. The leader had to apologize to Pullen and pay the court costs.[37]

The revelry associated with May Day celebrated not only the return of fertility to the earth and its crops but also the re-awakening of human passions and impulses. The divinations resorted to on May Eve have already been observed. On May Day the maypole would be erected in each village. The maypole usually made of birch wood, was a powerful sexual symbol of fertility, and the dancing and carol singing associated with the festival originally expressed these strong passions. One carol urged the young lovers to join in the merrymaking:

Cydgodwch, y meibion hyfrydol eu moddion,
Mae'r bedw'n bur leision, luosog fodd;
Pawb eled a'i fedwen i'w gariad eglurwen,
Ei seren fain, irwen, eurfodd.

Dancing around the May pole
(Mary Evans Picture Library)

A'r merched, ewch chwithe i'r gerddi i hel llysie,
Daw, yn siwr, eich cariade i'r dryse yn ddi-drai;
Ceisiwch yn gyfannedd i'r himpie paradwysedd
Weilch gweddedd, glan, dofedd, di-fai.[38]

(Arise together, young lads, pleasant their manner, The birch trees are quite green, and plentiful; Let each take his birch rod (see further, Chapter 6) to his radiant sweetheart, His precious, fresh, golden star. And you girls, go out into the gardens to gather herbs (perhaps a reference to some charm for divination?) Your lovers will surely flock to your doors. Seek pleasantly for the exquisite youths, Faultless, pure, gentle and comely suitors.)

Another May carol warns the young people of the intense and excessive passions sometimes aroused by May's beauty and freshness:

Gocheled pob merch dawel
Wrth wasgu a nesu yn isel,
I lencyn ar ei drafel
Roi, dan ei bogel, big;
Gwell cadw'r ddodren berffeth
Ar [ ] *nyd efo'r eneth*
Rhag myned i fwmio mameth,
Ysyweth, yn ei sig.[39]

(Let every quiet maiden beware lest Whilst cuddling and approaching low A young lad on his travels gives her a prick below her navel; It is better to keep the clothes perfect . . . with the girl rather than to go, alas, to play at motherhood . . .)

These pagan May Day festivities were not supplanted by Christian festivals but they were gradually christianized and in most of the carols which have survived the moral and religious references outweigh the original connections with fertility cults. Many of these May Day customs would be repeated on the Eve of St John at midsummer, especially in Glamorgan where the summer birch, *y fedwen haf*, was so popular.

As the crops ripened, towards the late summer months of July and August, the young people would begin to look forward to the hay harvest. Farmers would help one another to harvest their hay crops and it would be quite common to find up to forty

Hay-cocks at Brechfa, Dyfed c. 1900. Young maid-servants would be thrown down into the haycocks, cuddled and kissed by manservants during the hay harvest.

(Welsh Folk Museum)

Workers at the hay harvest at Pen-y-banc, Drefach-Felindre, Carmarthenshire (Dyfed) c. 1914-18. The hay harvest was an important social occasion with many young people, male and female, from different farms, working together.

(Welsh Folk Museum)

men and women working together in a hayfield. The young farm-servants naturally relished this chance to meet servants from other farms for, although the work would be laborious, the companionship of the hayfield was greatly treasured. This freedom of social intercourse gave rise to the custom of rolling and kissing in the hay. References to this ritual in England are scarce, although Arthur Munby, in his description of adult games at Crystal Palace, London, in 1859, mentions in passing 'the servant girl who rather enjoys being kissed in the hayfield',[40] and implies that it was a commonplace occurrence. Likewise in Wales, few references to the custom have survived outside south-west Wales, in the old counties of Pembroke, Cardigan and Carmarthen. One rather vague reference does occur in a ballad by Abel Jones or *Y Bardd Crwst*, a ballad-monger from Llanrwst, who spent most of his time travelling the fairs of Gwent and Glamorgan during the second half of the last century. In his song of praise to the farm-servants of Wales he mentions one Siani Dolgellau and her wanton ways:

Yr hon a fu'n dorog o'i meistr
Rol chware'r hen Jig yn y gwair.[41]

(she who became pregnant by her master After playing the old jig in the hay.)

However, he does not stipulate that Siani met her downfall during the hay harvest itself.

Most of the other references confirm the south-west connection, as in a ballad by Ywain Meirion, an earlier ballad-monger, who despite his name, was particularly associated with Glamorgan. In his song in praise of Welsh farmers, their man-servants and maids he says:

'Rol iddynt weithio'n galed mewn chwys a lludded lawn
Trwy'r flwyddyn ar ei gore o'r bore hyd brynhawn.
Cant weithia beth llawenydd mewn priodas neu ddydd ffair,
Ac yn Sir Aberteifi gyd-garu yn y gwair . . .[38]

(When they have toiled hard at their best in sweat and great fatigue, Throughout the year from morning until afternoon,They have joy sometimes in a wedding or on a fair day, And in Cardiganshire a frolic together in the hay.)

A Tudor woodcut of a hay harvest with a courting couple in the background.
(The Fotomas Index Picture Library)

The custom varied slightly from place to place, even within this confined area, and it has been fascinating to learn that at least nine dialectical terms were in common use. In the Cardigan area, if a man romped with a maid in full view of the others present, threw her into a haycock and kissed her it would be known as *ffocso* (from the English 'to fox'?).[43] The term in the Lampeter area was *torchi* (to roll); in Llandysul *twmlo* (to tumble); Tre-lech *rolio* (to roll) or *powto* (to pout); and in nearby Cwm-bach/Meidrim we hear of allowing '*pum munud i bowto*' (five minutes to pout) during the afternoon tea interval. In the Newport, Pembrokeshire, area it was called *whariad* (a frolicking). *Sicineia*, the term used in the Pembrey area, is not as easy to explain, but one can tentatively suggest that it is derived from 'kiss' or *cus(an)* and *cynhaeaf*, harvest, thus a 'harvest kiss'.[44] In eastern Dyfed, the Brynaman area it was simply called *awr ar y gwair* (an hour on the hay).[45]

The most difficult name to interpret was the one recorded from an informant in the Fishguard/Llanwnda area. Mr Johnny Miles described how, when the maid-servants brought tea out to the hayfield, the main farm-servant would seize one of them and *rhoi gringrown iddi,* (give her a *gringrown*). During the ritual, hay would be rubbed all over the girl so that he would *brwnti hi â gwair i gyd*, (dirty her all over with hay).[46] The term *gringrown* was obviously not a Welsh word although Mr Miles used it naturally in his dialect. Light was thrown on its meaning when it was recalled that in the English dialect of south Pembrokeshire the custom was called 'to give a green gown'; *rhoi gringrown* being a crude corruption of the English. Thus the description given by Mr Miles of the ritual of rubbing the girl with the fresh, green hay would seem to be particularly apt. According to *Tales and Traditions of Tenby*, 1858, if anybody entered a field at haymaking time:

> he or she was immediately pounced upon by the haymakers of the opposite sex, tossed about on the hay-cocks, and bound with hay-bands, till a species of blackmail had been levied . . . The ceremony when performed on females was termed 'giving them a green gown' and when on the other sex, 'stretching their backs'.[47]

It is also interesting to note that the term 'give her a green gown' was used as early as 1629 in an English love letter.[48]

A court case in Carmarthen in 1846, proves that men were also subjected to being 'foxed' or 'rolled' in the hay. A maid-servant, Eliza Evans, and her companions were brought before the court for 'rolling'. It seems that a local doctor and a police official had called at a hayfield and had been greeted boisterously by the girls working there. The doctor had realized at once what was afoot, and had escaped quickly, but the girls had seized the 'Captain' and rolled him well in the newly-mown hay. Then one of them tied his legs with a hay band. During the court case Dr Lawrence was called before the magistrates and he gave witness that rolling was an ancient custom and that he had been subjected to it twenty or thirty times previously. Accordingly, the girls were released and the Captain was ordered to pay the costs of the case, much to his embarrassment. On this occasion old usage proved too tenacious to be lightly dismissed, even by the new arm of the law.[49]

Indeed, this hayfield custom persisted well into the twentieth century. One informant could remember that it was usually *y gwas mawr* (the main farm-servant), who would take the leading role in the *ffocso*. He would choose a young maid, new to the customs of the hayfield, throw her down without ceremony into a haycock, kiss and fondle her. The informant felt that he witnessed the enactment of an ancient ritual which had implicit sexual undertones and which must have been linked with pagan fertility rites.[50]

A similar custom, though not as well documented, formed part of the corn harvest traditions. From Llansilin, Clwyd, a reference has survived to the custom of 'rolling the younger maid-servants (often helpers at harvest time) in the loose corn on the barn floor with attempts at kissing by the younger swains'.[51] Young lovers would certainly take advantage of the need to work in pairs to make *deise pen-lin* (knee sheaves) on the cornfield in the Gwaun Valley, Pembrokeshire, especially as the work would often continue into the early hours of the morning.[52] The spring and summer seasons would be popular for weddings and, once again, the rich array of customs associated with this rite of passage and the emotions released during such a ceremony, provided fertile ground for aspiring courting couples.[53]

The month of August brought with it a chance for further revelry and socializing, for the parishes would hold their *gwylmabsantau*, patronal festivals, during the summer. These festivals gained the reputation for being rallying points for 'disorderly people, bawling, drinking, singing, dancing'.[54] For this reason one can assume that they would have attracted young people from far and wide. It was probably a festive gathering of this nature which intrigued Richard Warner, who travelled through Wales in August 1789. At Pontneddfechan in the upper Neath Valley, he was invited to witness a 'genuine Welsh Ball', where a party of about twenty-five 'rustics' danced to the music of the village harp. 'On a sudden,' he observed, 'the dance ceased and the harper, running his finger rapidly down the chords of his instrument, gave the accustomed signal, on which every gentleman saluted his partner three or four times with considerable ardour.'[55] Such expressions of affection brought upon these merry gatherings the severe censure of nineteenth-century religious reformers. The Reverend David Davies, minister of Croes-y-parc Baptist chapel, Llanbedr-y-fro in the Vale of Glamorgan, 1852-7, took pride in the fact that he had succeeded in eliminating the local patronal festival which he considered to be 'a source of pollution for the youth of the area' and 'a hellish jubilee'.[56]

The summer months would also allow time for outdoor recreation. Young people from Crai, Breconshire, used to go on a pilgrimage to Llyn y Fan Fach, Carmarthenshire, on 1 August, 'Lammas tide', every year to see the apparition of the maiden of Llyn y Fan arise from the lake. As the journey was long it would be a nocturnal pilgrimage which would doubtless be 'characterized by no little immorality'.[57] Indeed *c.* 1850 two lads who had joined the pilgrimage quarelled over a girl and in the ensuing skirmish, fell to their deaths down the mountain side.[58]

The young people of Upper Cwmtawe loved to walk on the Brecon Beacons during early August too, as the local rhymester Joseph Thomas, Y Felin, commented:

> The young people find joy out walking,
> Nothing worries them while they have their hands free,
> But they follow their noses up to the Beacons
> To see the lakes, the still water.
>
> (translation)

Dyfnallt (1873-1956) could recall seeing hoards of Cwmllynfell youths in the same area proceeding towards Fforch Aman Well and the young people of Penrhiw-fawr nearby making for Gellionnen Well.[59] Likewise, until the 1920s of this century, young men and girls, from Tirabad in the north to Cwm Cilienu in the south, used to meet on the nearest Sunday to August Bank holiday at Drelaeth Well on the Epynt Mountains in Breconshire, and many a young lad met his lover during this excursion.[60] A similar pilgrimage takes place in North Wales today, for, during the nine-day full moon period towards the end of September, young people in the Snowdonia area gather to climb Snowdon to marvel at the sunrise. The last bus from Caernarfon to Llanberis can be full on the Saturday night, and very many couples join the merry band of walkers, as the custom gives them a useful excuse for being together all through the night.[61]

One of the adult games played on such outings as these was 'kiss in the ring', involving men and women chasing and saluting one another. Frances Place noticed it at the Great Easter Greenwich Fair in the 1820s, whilst Arthur Munby found masses of youths playing it at Crystal Palace in 1861. He describes how he saw them play '[A] nice looking girl came up and saying 'Are you in the ring Sir?' offered me her favour—a leaf. I acquiesced,; I caught and led and kissed her; and stimulated by the feat we joined in the game.'[62] This was a children's game in Llandegla yn Ial at the end of the last century, a game played at nutting and crab apple gathering time. Here the game was played on the village square and, if a boy successfully chose a girl once, he would probably try to choose her again when his chance came. Little by little the group dissolved into couples and the couples into sweethearts.[63] This game became popular in later times on Sunday School outings at Whitsuntide. The Sunday schools of the Vales of Dulais and Tawe,Glamorganshire, used to meet on Y Coelbren on Whit Monday and after the children had played all morning, the young people would catch the train to Coelbren junction at about 5 o'clock. Once there, they would proceed to Cae Penrhyn, form two circles, one for the girls, the other for the boys, and play kiss-in-the-ring. Many marriages sprang from this innocent beginning.[64]

As has been noted, the traditional popular recreational activities, the fairs, May Day frolics and patronal festivities were being rigorously criticized by religious reformers during the second half of the nineteenth century as depraved and disreputable gatherings. During the same period more and more young people were becoming involved as nonconformists in activities centred upon religious meetings. The numerous Sunday services, coupled with the many weekday evening meetings, prayer meetings, singing practices, *seiadau* (fellowships), the Band of Hope, and so forth, ensured that chapels grew to be 'the chief centres of organized recreation in rural Wales'.[65] Young people would dress in their Sunday best for these occasions and spend much of their time gauging the 'talent value' of their place of worship. There was nothing startlingly new in this, of course, for Dafydd ap Gwilym, our pre-eminent medieval love poet, admitted that his main reason for attending the service at Llanbadarn Fawr church, Cardiganshire, was to admire and assess the beautiful local girls:

> In Llanbadarn every Sunday
> Was I, and (judge who may)
> Towards chaste girls I faced,

My nape to a God rightly chaste,
And through my plumes gazed long
At that religious throng . . .

Poor Dafydd had little to show for his efforts at the end of the service, except a stiff neck:

I'm finished, I'm too late,
Wry-necked without a mate.[66]

As early as the year 1847, the prejudiced Commissioners responsible for the infamous *Commission of Inquiry into the State of Education in Wales* had begun to worry about the social and moral consequences of over-zealous chapel attendance:

The great number of nightly prayer meetings and Pwncau schools lead to bad results: they are places at which lovers agree to meet, and from which they return together at late hours. At these schools (Sunday Schools) young persons of both sexes are congregated together in great numbers and in close contact.[67]

Because of this a disapproving correspondent to the *Carmarthen Weekly Reporter* in 1901 commented:

Sunday 'is called the Lord's Day, but in Carmarthen, it is par excellence, the Devil's day.'

In larger villages and towns a custom developed to further advance courting facilities and opportunities amongst the young people. After the Sunday evening service the youths of all denominations used to congregate in small groups in the streets. Then they would begin to walk, or parade, towards a specific destination perhaps a mile or two away. In some areas the boys would walk on one side of the road and the girls on the other, while it was also common to see a row of boys following a row of girls. In Pontarddulais, all the young people would walk up the road towards Swansea and stop to turn around on the brow of the hill descending into the village of Pont-lliw. In Penderyn, the known courting couples would go up Penderyn road while the unattached youths strolled down towards the Rhigos.[68]

As young people were allowed greater social freedom from about 1890 until World War II, the custom of parading the streets became the adopted practice on Saturday evenings too. Youths flocked into the small towns to join in the ritual:

> One of the strangest customs among the young crowd while they searched for sweethearts was to walk in one interminable circle around the streets of Pwllheli, on Saturday nights. From the Maes, up Penlan and then along the main street and turning down Stryd Moch back towards the Maes—or going in the other direction—this was the usual route, and this custom continues to some extent today (1984). One of the names for this was *mynd i weindio'r cloc* (going to wind the clock), another *mynd i lyfnu* (going to level?) . . .[69]

The same Welsh term *llyfnu* was common in Anglesey too;[70] while in Powys the name *sodli*, to heel, describes how the boys tried to attract the attention of the girls walking in front of them by catching the heels of their shoes.[71]

The most common terms for the custom both in north and south Wales were borrowed from the English, for it was variously called 'the monkey parade' as in Pontarddulais, 'the bunny run' as in Morriston, Swansea, or the 'monkey run'. In Caernarfon, the monkey run would involve two or three trips around the main streets of the town on both Saturday night and *nos Sadwrn bach* (little Saturday night, that is, Wednesday night). When the parade eventually arrived at the Maes, *y mŵf* (the move) would take place—as the boys jostled for a sweetheart—and soon couples would be seen *yn walio* (walling), courting against the quay wall.[72] The monkey run is found in a modified form in Caernarfon today amongst the youths who are too young to go to pubs and clubs. In Swansea young people indulge in the 'Pick n Mix' as they saunter up and down the Kingsway on a Saturday night.

The conventions of the Welsh parades were not as elaborate as those of the larger cities of England where 'everyone obeyed the codes of the "Monkey rank"'.[73] In Manchester's Oldham Street, for example:

> From Hulme, from Ardwick, and from Ancoats they came, in the main well dressed, and frequently sporting a flower in the button-holes of their jacket. But the motive is not so much that of meeting

> their friends, as of forming an acquaintanceship with some young girl. Girls resort to Oldham Street on a Sunday night in nearly as large numbers as the boys . . . The boys exchange rough salutations with the girls, who seem in no way less vigorous than the boys themselves, and whose chief desire, one would think, was to pluck from the lads' buttonholes, the flowers which many of them wear.[74]

Each promenade had its own age and social geography. In Preston, the Fishergate run attracted the better class of older apprentices and shop assistants, while the younger lads of a lower social order attended the Avenham and Miller Parks parades.[75]

Gradually, during the second quarter of the twentieth century, the chapel began to loose its grip upon organized recreation for young people with cultural evenings, *eisteddfodau* and *twmpathau dawns* (folk dances) gaining in popularity. It became socially acceptable to see two young people courting in public and should the young lovers wish for more privacy they could seek the back row of the pictures or court in the car. Indeed the more respectable were horrified at the thought of the young people flocking to the cinemas, not because of the content of the films but because they allowed young men and women to sit together in comparative comfort in the dark.[76] Due to the impact of two World Wars, the fabric of society changed immensely in the field of courtship rituals and customs, as in all other aspects of life. Young people no longer had to wait upon organized festivals and calendrical activities to provide them with opportunities for casual acquaintanceships without commitment, or for the experiences of experimental courting relationships.

NOTES

[1]*Royal Commission on Labour. The Agricultural Labourer,* Vol.ii, *Wales,* 1893, pp.166, 115.

[2]Ibid., p.11.

[3]*Y Beirniad,* vol. 19, 1878, p.363.

[4]P.J.Donovan, (edit.) *Cywyddau Serch y Tri Bedo* (Cardiff, 1982), p.15.

[5]*Cymru,* vol. 19, 1900, p.229.

[6]Tegwyn Jones, *Baledi Ywain Meirion* (Llyfrau'r Faner, 1980), p.26.

[7]W.F.M. Mss 1737/16.

[8]Catrin Stevens, 'Welsh Love Story', *Country Quest,* March 1978, p.14.
[9]Oral testimony, Eluned Jones, Boncath.
[10]Ben Evans, *Cerddi'r Cerwyn* (Whitland, 1927), p.9.
[11]Stevens, p.15.
[12]*Lleuad Yr Oes*, 1828.
[13]Trefor M Owen, 'Caru yn y Ffeiriau yn y Ganrif ddiwetha', *Medel,* vol.2, 1985, p.43.
[14]Sain Record 1164 M. Traddodiad Gwerin Cymru 2, Accompanying notes by D Roy Saer, p.10.
[15]David Jenkins, *The Agricultural Community in South West Wales at the turn of the twentieth century* (Cardiff, 1971), p.125.
[16]Daniel E Jones, *Hanes Plwyfi Llangeler a Phenboyr* (Llandysul, 1899), p.369.
[17]John Bevan, 'Astudiaeth Seinyddol o Gymraeg Llafar Coety Walia a Rhuthun ym Mro Morgannwg', Unpublished M.A.Thesis (Univ. of Wales), 1970, vol.ii, pp.431, 544, 726.
[18]W J Davies, pp. 239-40.
[19]*Seren Gomer,* vol.16, 1832, p.322.
[20]*Cymdeithas y Traethodau Crefyddol,* no.33, *Llanw Llŷn,* 96, Nov. 1984.
[21]Huw Walters, 'Chwifio Baner Dirwest: Cenhadaeth Dafydd Daniel Amos', *Cof Cenedl V*, edit. Geraint H Jenkins (Llandysul 1990) p.93.
[22]Dylan Thomas, *Under Milk Wood* (Denb. 1954), p.66.
[23]*Royal Commission on Labour,* pp.151-2.
[24]R W Malcolmson, *Popular Recreations in English Society, 1700-1850* (Cambridge, 1973), p.78.
[25]E Tegla Davies, *Gyda'r Blynyddoedd* (Liverpool, 1952), p.119.
[26]T Gwynn Jones, p. 187.
[27]*Cambro-Briton*, 1822.
[28]Huw Walters, *Canu'r Pwll a'r Pulpud* (Denbigh, 1987), p. 284.
[29]Trefor M Owen, *A Pocket Guide to the Customs and Traditions of Wales* (Cardiff, 1991), p.53.
[30]Hugh Evans, *The Gorse Glen,* a translation of the Welsh *Cwm Eithin*, by E Morgan Humphreys, (Liverpool, 1948), pp.147-8.
[31]Rhiannon Ifans, *Sêrs a Rybana, Astudiaeth o'r Canu Gwasael* (Gomer, 1983), p.65.
[32]Testimony of Glan Richards, 61 Heol Rudd, Carmarthen, 1984.
[33]Ifans, p.136.
[34]Ibid., p.146.
[35]see Chapter 8.
[36]Trefor M Owen, *Welsh Folk Customs* (Cardiff, 1959, Third Edition 1974), pp.89-90.
[37]John R Gillis, *For Better for Worse* (Oxford 1985), p. 25.
[38]Ifans, p.195.
[39]Ibid.
[40]Gillis, p.23.
[41]Bangor Mss xxii, 151.
[42]Tegwyn Jones, p.26.
[43]Jenkins, p.91.
[44]Oral testimony gathered in West Dyfed, 1976.
[45]Trefor M Owen, *A Pocket Guide* . . . ., p. 15.
[46]Oral testimony, Johnny Miles, Goodwick, Fishguard, 1976.
[47]*Tales and Traditions of Tenby,* pp.24-5; *Pembrokeshire County Guardian,* Oct. 2, 1897.
[48]Alan Macfarlane, *Marriage and Love in England, 1300-1840* (Oxford, 1986).

[49]*Yr Haul,* 1846, p.272; Elfyn Scourfield, 'Y Mudiad Diweirdeb', *Y Genhinen,* vol.28, 1978, pp.104-5.

[50]T Llew Jones, 'Gŵyl Awst', *Llafar Gwlad,* Eisteddfod Abergwaun, 1986, p.7; Oral testimony, T Llew Jones, 1986.

[51]*Bye-gones,* 31 Oct., 1928.

[52]*Llyfr Lloffion Cwmgwaun a'r Cylch,* vol ii; Peggy Williams, 1984, p.95.

[53]Elias Owen, 'On some customs still remaining in Wales', *Y Cymmrodor,* vol.ii., 1878, p.137.

[54]G J Williams, 'Glamorgan Customs in the Eighteenth Century', *Gwerin,* vol.1, 1951, p.99f.

[55]Rev Richard Warner, *A Second Walk Through Wales* (London, 1799), pp.114-116.

[56]John Bevan, 'Mabsant Llanbad', *Medel,* vol.2, 1985, p.11.

[57]T Llew Jones, 'Gŵyl Awst', p.6.

[58]Trefor M Owen, *What Happened to Welsh Folk Customs',* The Katherine Briggs Lecture, No. 4 (London 1985).

[59]Huw Walters, *Canu'r Pwll a'r Pulpud,* . . . p. 282.

[60]John H Davies, 'Ffynnon Drelaeth ac eraill', *Llafar Gwlad,* no.14. 1986-7, p.15.

[61]Twm Elias, 'Dywediadau am y Tywydd', *Llafar Gwlad,* no.10, 1985-6, p.4.

[62]Gillis, p.23.

[63]E Tegla Davies, p.58.

[64]Oral testimony, Mrs Rhiannon Jones, 2 Bishop's Walk, Morriston, Swansea.

[65]*Welsh Rural Communities* (Cardiff, 1960), editorial preface by Elwyn Davies, p.xi.

[66]*The Penguin Book of Welsh Verse,* translated by A Conran (Great Britain, 1967), p.141.

[67]*Report of the Commission of Inquiry into the State of Education in Wales, 1847.* Part I, p.254.

[68]Oral Testimony, Nancy Selwood, Penderyn.

[69]Twm Elias, 'Llen Gwerin', *Llanw Llyn,* 97, Dec. 1984.

[70]W H Roberts, 'Ebra Nhw a Mynta Fi', *Bro'r Eisteddfod 3, Ynys Mon,* edit. by Bedwyr Lewis Jones and Derec Llwyd Morgan (Llandybïe 1983) p.36.

[71]Oral testimony, Enid Pierce Roberts, Bangor, 1984.

[72]Oral testimony, Richard Hughes, Y Co bach, Caernarfon, 1986.

[73]Gillis, p.271.

[74]C E B Russell, *Manchester Boys* (Manchester, 1905), pp.115-116; Gillis, p.271.

[75]Gillis, pp. 271-2.

[76]Dafydd Roberts, 'Y Deryn Nos a'i Deithiau', Diwylliant Derbyniol Chwarelwyr Gwynedd, *Cof Cenedl,* cyf. 3, gol. Geraint H. Jenkins (Llandysul, 1988), t.160.

Chapter 3

'Under the Eaves'

Once the young lads had succeeded, whether on the hayfield, in the fair or during the May Day revelries perhaps, to assess the local girls and to strike up an acquaintance with one of their choice, they could hope to pursue their suit further by arranging a date *oed* or an appointment *pwynt/points* to meet again. Yet, as has been emphasized, within the rural, agricultural community the young maidens would not be allowed, especially during the darker winter months, to wander freely to fulfil such engagements. Aspiring lovers had no choice but to try to court the girls at their own homes or places of employment, under the closed, but knowing, eyes of their elders. The alleged secrecy of this form of courtship was doubtless one of its main attractions.[1].

For convenience, and company, young men would often venture on courting missions in pairs, or as courting parties, *gwŷr caru*. These groups would also return together in the early hours of the morning, and it is hardly surprising that these were the ones who told blood-curdling tales of seeing ghosts, apparitions, corpse-candles and phantom funerals on their travels.[2] Some hopeful lovers roamed from one farm to another with no set destination, trying to curry some girls' favours before the night was out. Twm Rhos Mawn found that the girls considered his attitude to courtship rather too cavalier:

> During his second year as manservant Twm began to go out at night courting . . . at last I had a chance to join him . . . We started out together, one evening, soon after ten . . . After walking for about a mile and a half we came to a farm called Bryn Clogwyn; there were two very smart girls at Bryn Clogwyn, but they were too wise to come to the window that evening, although we knocked our best. Thence, we went to Llanerch Goch, there was only one daughter here and Twm wasn't too sure in which loft she slept; but we took a chance and knocked on the first window. The window opened immediately but rather than a chat with Marged we were greeted by a volcano's lava . . . and the father poured upon us the most eloquent censure I have ever heard . . . including threats and

> slaughter, and finishing his speech by calling to the dog 'Pero, Pero, Pero, go after them boy!' . . . We proceeded towards Y Cleidir. In Y Cleidir two of the loveliest local girls lived. Jane, the eldest, came to the window at the first fistful of soil. 'Good evening,' said Twm, 'Would it be possible to speak to Elizabeth Huws?' But Elizabeth wouldn't come into sight. 'She won't get up,' said Jane, returning to the window, 'but perhaps you wouldn't mind talking to me instead of my sister'. 'No indeed, I wouldn't,' replied Twm, 'it'll all be the same at the end'. 'Oh! and if so' she replied, 'go home then, you wouldn't mind someone else instead of me', and she closed the window with a bang. Twm didn't seem inclined to knock anywhere else that evening.[3]

But Twm did manage to avenge this insult by taking a water pistol with him on his next visit to Y Cleidir!

Most of the young lads did have a definite destination, however, and some would try to ensure a favourable reception by corresponding beforehand. A letter from J Jenkins of Pentre-felin, in August 1877, to arrange such a meeting, has been preserved at the Welsh Folk Museum and displays a quaint contrast between the formality of its style and the familiarity of its content. He addresses Miss Williams as a very respectable young lady and then goes on to urge her to open the door to him and to spend the whole night in his company.[4] James Evans, in his love letters to Mary Williams, farm-servant at Castle Morris, Pembrokeshire, *c.* 1890, emphasized that he had to walk seven miles from Southwood, Roch, to visit her and that he felt morally entitled for his effort to be well received:

> i am comming down about a week befor the fair, it will be cold then . . . an i am so tender remember if i will come an nock at the window i hope that you will take pity on me that you come down an turn the poor little boy in.

In another letter he goes further, for he not only arranges his own *oed* but that of their respective friends, for he urges Mary:

> to tell the girl is with you that i am comming up with a chap with me next time an you can tell her that he is a good one to rub a bit on the leg an perhaps on something elch (else) for a bit of fun.[5]

Perhaps it would have benefited James Evans to have heeded the advice in the traditional verse:

Nid af i garu byth ond hynny,
A chydymaith hefo myfi,
Rhag ofn iddo brofi'n ffalsiwr,—
Dwyn fy mwyd oddi ar fy nhreinsiwr![6]

(I shall never go courting again, With a fellow-courter, Lest he proves to be a cheat,—Stealing my food from on my platter!)

Even on informal courting visits, the social structure had to be strictly maintained. A farmer's son would be expected to join the servant lads on a night visit, for if he did not there was thought to be something wrong with his masculinity. But once at the farmhouse the son would pay court to the daughter of the household while the servant would seek out the maid.[7]

Experienced lovers might choose to take a young lad as company when courting. This would be the *gwas caru* (the servant in courtship) and his task would be to serve his master and remove any obstructions to courtship. When Dafydd ap Gwilym wanted to win his dear Enid's favours during the local patronal festival at Rhosyr, Anglesey, he sent his servant to her loft with a drink of wine. She, however, rejected his advances and even belittled his servant by pouring the wine over his hair. The next time, Dafydd muttered bitterly, this girlfriend would only get 'a spoonful of warm water' from his servant.[8] The *gwas caru* might also serve as an intermediary in cases of negotiations and quarrels between such lovers. Certainly this was the role Roger Lowe, a Lancashire mercer's apprentice and diarist in the 1660s, performed for his friends and they for him.[9] According to William Williams, a native of Llansannan, Clwyd, who died in 1917, many suitors in the early part of the last century would go courting on horseback and the *gwas caru* would also be mounted as a matter of display and to impress the girls.[10] The custom of enlisting the help and support of an attendant was still practised in rural Carmarthenshire at the beginning of the twentieth century and such an arrangement was regarded by many as an apprenticeship in the art of courting at night. It was while fulfilling this role that Ifan Ffatri Isha first drew the attention of Ann Davies, a young maid at Mwche farm, near Llan-gain, *c.*1911. At this farm

> There were iron bars, as thick as a blacksmith's thumb accross the windows of the maids' room. When the lads came courting they had to throw gravel at the glass until one of the girls opened the window and welcomed the lover. Then, a ladder against the wall, and up the boy would shin for a chat and a quick kiss between the bars.
>
> It was Ifan's responsibility to hold the ladder steady and keep watch for the Master. But the courting continued for far too long and the *gwas caru*'s head fell lower and lower until he was fast asleep on the lowest rung of the ladder. At Mwche there was quite a stupid billy goat and when it saw the *gwas caru*'s head lowering, the billy goat took it as a threat. Its head went down and up it came like the wind, butting Ifan and the ladder half way up the yard, leaving the lover hanging like a piece of ivy from the window bars.[11]

Fortunately, Ifan Ffatri Isha had glimpsed his future bride through the window and in spite of his escapade he was soon back in his own right as a fully-fledged suitor at Mwche Farm.

Doubtlessly, the courtship attendant also provided company for a lover as he trudged the tedious miles from his own home or place of employment to hers. One ardent young lad from Cwm-rheidol chose to walk fifteen miles to pursue his suit and, to show their appreciation of his devotion, the family lent him a horse for his journey home. Rather unfortunately, however, the lover felt that the horse offered a better bargain than the girl and neither he nor the horse were ever heard of again![12] It was considered to be unwise to court too near home[13] and it was said of one who did wander far afield in search of girls that he had *gwlan hwrdd yn sodlau ei esgidiau* (ram's wool in the soles of his shoes).[14] One old rhyme emphasized the wisdom of casting widely for a sweetheart:

> *Caru Nghaer a charu Nghorwen,*
> *Caru draw dan Graig y Dderwen,*
> *Caru wedyn dros y mynydd,*
> *Cael yng Nghynwyd gariad newydd.*[15]

(Courting at Chester and courting at Corwen, Courting over there under Graig y Dderwen, Courting next over the mountain, Finding a new girlfriend in Cynwyd.)

while another predicted woe from roaming too far:

Yn awr, 'rwyf wedi drysu,
Wrth gerdded i hir garu,
Er bod y merched yn dra rhwydd
Mi rof y swydd i fyny.[16]

(I am totally confused Through walking far to court,Though the girls are quite easy I shall give up this practice.)

Yet there is plenty of evidence that roaming freely and extensively in search of a young woman was disapproved of strongly, especially by local lads. A 'cockerel from another parish' was a very unwelcome intruder, and his trespassing was considered to be an insult to local manhood and prowess. This is the full impact of the last lines of the popular folk song:

Os nghariad ddaw 'ma heno
I guro'r gwydyr glas,
Rhowch ateb gweddus iddo,
Na ddwedwch ddim yn gas, -
Nad ydyw'r ferch ddim gartref
Na'i hwyllys da'n y tŷ,
Llanc ifanc o blwyf arall
Sydd wedi mynd â hi.[17]

(If my lover comes here tonight To knock at the blue glass,
Give him a seemly answer, Don't say anything nastily,—
That the girl is not at home, Neither is her good will in the house,For a young lad from another parish, Has taken her away.)

Such intruders would be coarsely treated in England. Strangers were fined a 'footing' of a shilling in the west and north, while in Yorkshire they could be 'packsheeted', tossed in a blanket, before being run out of the neighbourhood. The local girls expressed their anger too by calling such interlopers names and reciting derogatory and unsavoury verses about them. Trespassers who dared venture into the parish of Gravely in Hertfordshire were treated in a most humiliating way by exposing their backsides to a whirling grindstone and grinding them.[18] Likewise, in Montgomeryshire the intruder would be threatened:

on his way home he might be waylaid; pelted with clods, rolled in mud, or even tarred and feathered by a group of hooligans.[19]

Evidence of such extreme behaviour against a stranger is rare in Wales, though it is obvious that horseplay was common. The poor victim might be driven away or a disturbance caused outside the house he had visited. One young lad from Llanfallteg dared court a maid at the neighbouring parish of Efail-wen. He travelled there on an ass and left it, while he was courting, in the barn nearby. Sometime in the early hours of the morning he decided to return home and went in search of the ass. He found it marooned in the hayloft, too terrified to move. How he managed to persuade the ass to come down remained a mystery in the neighbourhood for years.[20] Likewise in north Wales, when a young lad from Glyndyfrdwy began courting a girl from Dinmael, the local youths decided to show their disapproval by hiding his motorbike in a field of oats. He had to walk home from his date that evening and return the next day amidst great teasing and derision in search of his bike.[21]

The severest censure was reserved in the Ceiriog valley, however, not for the trespassing youth but for the local girl who dared belittle the parish youths. She would be observed very carefully and her courtship would be subject to continuous malicious gossip. Even the young men's mothers joined in the criticism, predicting misfortune and shame upon her for her arrogance and affectation. And, if this pressure did not succeed, the locals would decide upon further and more drastic action:

> At a time when the girl would be dressed in her best finery, the lads sought a chance to *rhythu* her. They would surround the girl against her will, each one would grasp the brim of her hat firmly with his teeth, then they would open their trousers and each one would pass water on her dress, wetting all around her. Then they would loosen their grip on her hat and walk and run after her, mocking and shouting as they went.[22]

Is there perhaps some symbolic link between this strange Dyffryn Ceiriog custom and the tradition found in Tywyn, Merionethshire, on 1 May each year, for every young lad to throw a bucketful of water over his chosen girlfriend? This custom was popular until 1832 but during that year one girl suffered such a shock from the effect of the unexpected drenching that she died and the custom was immediately abolished.[23].

To explain this behaviour as merely an expression of jealousy towards trespassing suitors, especially when, as frequently occurred, none of the local lads had any interest in the local girl themselves, would be too simplistic. It seems more probable that such groups of youths considered themselves as custodians of local customs, and that it was their responsibility, therefore, to punish those who transgressed these traditions. Certainly this was the case in Sweden, Switzerland and other parts of central Europe where the young men's guilds fulfilled such a role.[24]

Eventually, when a courtship had continued for some time, hositility towards the interloping lover would cease and the stranger would be accepted. He might then venture to join the local lads to court once or twice a week, usually on the same night or nights, called *'Y Noson'*. The choice of night varied from locality to locality; some preferred Sundays:

> *Och a fi, ac och a finnau,*
> *Mor anaml y daw'r Suliau.*
> *Pe bai 'ngbariad i yn agos,*
> *Byddai'n Sul bob dydd o'r wythnos.*[25]

(Woe unto me, woe unto me; How unoften Sundays come. If my dearest were nearer, It would be Sunday every day of the week.)

Courting on Sunday evenings could present problems, as James Evans suggests in his letter to Mary Williams of Castle Morris; for he intended in future

> to come on a saturday night than sunday because i was taired last time; i was up before i had rest; i was home when the clock strike six o'clock an i had a cup of tea an off to my work.[26]

Indeed, it seems that Saturday night was the traditional courting night in Pembrokeshire.[27]

The actual process of courting at the young girl's residence in secrecy at night has already been suggested in some of the references quoted above. The young lover would arrive late in the evening, when the house would be in darkness and try to attract the attention of his intended by throwing gravel, sand and pebbles against her window. This custom has, therefore, been variously called *y cynnig* (the attempt) in Llŷn and Meirioneth,[28] *streicio* (striking) in Anglesey,[29] to be *ar y criws*, (on the cruise) in the Vale of Teifi,[30] but most commonly *mynd i gnocio/cnocio*, (to go knocking) in south Wales. This is the term found in the traditional verses:

Cyn caffael rhaid yw ceisio,
Cyn agor rhaid yw cnocio;
Ac os chwenychir afal per,
Mae'n rhaid mewn amser ddringo.

(Before finding one must search, Before opening, one has to knock; And if one desires a sweet apple, Eventually one must climb.)

Cnocio wnes i at Wen lliw'r blode;
Fe ddweda'i mam nad oedd hi gartre.
Mi'i canfum hi wrth olau'r lleuad,
Ar y llawr yn camu'i llygad.[31]

(I knocked on Gwen [the colour of flowers]; Her mother maintained that she wasn't at home. I caught a glimpse of her by the moonlight, On the ground floor giving me the glad eye.)

Another popular Welsh folk song imitates the sound of the gravel falling, pitter patter, on the window pane:

Titrwm, tatrwm, Gwen lliw'r ŵy,
Ni alla i'n hwy mo'r curo;
Mae'r gwynt yn oer oddi ar y llyn;
Lliw blodau'r dyffryn, deffro.
Chwyth y tân i gynnau toc—
Mae hi'n ddrycinog heno.[32]

(Pitter patter, Gwen, the colour of egg, I cannot carry on knocking; The wind is cold from over the lake, The colour of valley flowers, awaken. Fan the fire alight soon—It is stormy tonight.)

That this was the correct and customary procedure whilst courting at night is emphasized by the survival of two similar though independent folk tales, about two well-known characters within their own localities; Twm Weunbwll of Efail-wen, Dyfed, and Elis Bryn-du from the Corwen, Clwyd, area. Both Twm and Elis were bachelors and their mothers were equally concerned that they seemed to have little interest in the search for a wife. Thus they decided to teach their sons the age-long craft of courting at night and sent them both out into the dark with a fistful of gravel each and instructed them to throw the gravel up against the loft window. This part of the initiation ceremony was completed successfully and in both cases the mother opened the window and shouted down 'Who's there?' Both sons destroyed the atmosphere completely by replying quite unabashedly, 'But you know very well who's here Mam, it was you who sent me out!'[33]

Thus the young man would find himself *dan y pared* or *dan y bargod* (under the eaves) awaiting his lover's response. *Canu dan bared*, serenading the girl under her window, became a popular convention in medieval Welsh poetry. The poets describe themselves loitering with intent, in the most inclement weather under the girl's window; as in this fine *cywydd* (strict metre verse) by Dafydd ab Edmwnd:

Dyn wyf yn cerdded y nos;
Dedwyddach oedd dŷ diddos . . .
Dyn ni bu ar dyno bach
Dan bared wyneb oerach.

Deffro, fun, differ f'enaid;
Duw! dyn blin sy dan dy blaid . . .
Dig wyf yn arwain dy gerdd
Dan fargod, yn ofergerdd.
Drwy'r ffenestr dyro ffunen
Dy fam hael i doi fy mhen.[34]

(I'm a man walking the night; A snug house would be happier .. Sorry little wretch under a wall, there was never a colder face. Wake up, girl, protect my soul, A weary godly man's under your wall . . . (or according to above reading: God! the man under your wall is weary) Indignantly I bear your song, Under eaves vainly singing. Pass your kind mother's kerchief through the window to roof my head.)[35]

Neither rain nor snow could dampen these poets' ardour, though Dafydd ap Edmwnd couldn't resist reminding Cari Mwyn that he was suffering extreme discomfort for his true love:

er dy fwyn yr ydwyf fi
mewn eira yma yn oeri
dyred, fy nhraed a oerais
dyro dy ben drwy dy bais
a'th law yn un o'th lewys
ac a'r llall agor y llys.[36]

(it is for your sake that I am here, getting colder in the snow. Come, my feet have grown cold, put your head through your petticoat and your hand in one of your sleeves and with the other open up the court.)

Poor Bedo Aeddren, another late fifteenth-century poet complained bitterly that he had cold feet *allan heb na thân na thŷ* (out without fire or roof)[37], while Dafydd ap Gwilym, during one of his innumerable courting missions found his favourite spot under the eaves obstructed by *rhywlyb bibonwy* (a very wet icicle)![38] The 'obstacles theme', describing the frustrations and impediments that could sabotage a lovers' meeting is one of the most productive and dynamic themes in medieval Welsh love poetry.

Occasionally, the girls would prove impossible to awaken:

Curo y bum yn anial ffest
Yn ffenest' onest eneth
Methu'n wir ei deffro hi
A wnaeth i mi fynd ymeth.
Bydd yr hin yn rhewi'r haf
Pan geisiaf nesaf nosweth.[39]

(I knocked very vigorously On the honest wench's window,
Failing completely to waken her Made me go away.
It will be freezing in the summer When I try next for a night (with her).)

Câl nosweth (to have a night) was one of the terms used for courting the night. One rhymester vowed he would have no further dealings with such uncooperative maidens:

Nid af i garu byth ond hynny
At y merched trwm eu cysgu;
Af at lodes groenwen gryno
'N llawr y dyffryn, hawdd ei deffro.[40]

(I shall not bother to go courting again To the heavy-eyed maidens; I shall visit the shapely whiteskinned girl On the valley floor, she is easy to waken.)

Sometimes, the aspiring lover would find that he had arrived too late, and that another had usurped his position, while some would have to put up with a great deal of bantering and provoking from the girls before they would agree to proceed with the courting. The outcome of such flirting would not always be to the boy's advantage:

Fy nghariad annwyl dyner, glws,
Tyrd i'r ffenest neu i'r drws.
Mae gŵr ifanc dan y pared
Yn dymuno cael dy weled.

Yn wir ni chodaf i o'm gwely
I siarad gwagedd drwy'r ffenestri.
Mae'r gwynt yn oer, a minnau'n dene
Dowch yn gynt neu sefwch gartre.[41]

(My pretty, tender dear love, Come to the window or the door. There's a young lad under the eaves Wishing to see you.
Indeed I shall not get out of my bed To talk idly through the windows. The wind is chilly and I am thin. Come earlier or stay at home!)

An excellent example of this kind of battle of wits, reminiscent, of course, of wassailing songs with their emphasis upon the inclement weather, the distance to be walked and the need to waken the participants,[42] is found in an old folk-song collected by J Ffos Davies of Felin-fach, Cardiganshire, from a native of the area in about 1880. The songster describes how he went courting one night and knocked at the young lady's window, above the parlour:

Atebai y ferch, do, cyn pen ychydig,
'Pwy wyt ti y bachgen a'th siarad gwenieithlyd,
A phwy rwyt yn mofyn; a phle rwyt yn myned,
Gan ddweyd y fath eiriau mewn siarad mor fwyned.'

Tydi rwyf yn mofyn—a thi rwyf yn garu
Os caf fi ddod mewn a chael dy gwmni
[Alternative reading: 'ac atat i'r gwely']
Waeth atat ti'n unig y mae fy nymuniad
O dattod dy gloion a rho im dderbyniad

(The girl answered, indeed, within a little while, 'Who are you, the boy with the silver tongue, And who do you want, and where are you going, Saying such words in such a fine language'
It's you I want—it's you I love. If I can come in and have your company, [Alternative reading 'and with you to bed'] Since my wish is to come to you only. Oh unfasten your locks and receive me in.)

The girl, however, was not so easily flattered for she asked him where he had been courting the night before Whit Sunday? In the next verse the boy denies the accusation and maintains it to be the idle talk of a rival. The girl cannot accept this and refuses to talk further to such a 'blackguard'. Undaunted, the young lover saunters away; but not before throwing his last punch into the courting arena:

Mi glywais fod gennyt rhyw fachgen ag arian
Yn awr yn dy garu, nid tlawd fel fy hunan.
Pob lwc iti, Elin, Pob lwc wrth roi ffarwel,
At arall mi af, wrth fy modd rwyn ymadael.[43]

(I've heard that you've got a moneyed young lad Now in love with you, not a poor man like me. Good luck to you, Elin, Good luck as we farewell, I shall go to another, I shall depart at my will.)

Many an unwanted suitor would return home rejected and dejected from these night visits. It is easy to imagine the dismay of one young lad who had striven his utmost to win the favour of an attractive, young maid-servant at Bodfel near Llannor, Llŷn, only to be received not by her open arms as expected, but by a shower of excrement from the chamber pot![44]

Certain elements of the custom of serenading 'under the eaves' are found in the famous fourteenth-century *marwnad*, elegy, by Llywelyn Goch ap Meurig Hen to the fair Lleucu Llwyd of Pennal, Merioneth. We see the poet approach the girl's home (symbolically the grave); he loiters falteringly, 'walking to and fro in the cold', under her window and urges her to arise (from the grave) to open the 'black earth-door' for him. Throughout the poem faint doubts linger as to whether Lleucu is indeed dead and buried or whether it is her love for the poet that has so cruelly and completely evaporated. In the very last line of the poem the mention of a *clicied* (latch), suggesting perhaps that Lleucu could, if she wished, raise the latch and receive the poet after all, suspends the belief and the very last greeting to Lleucu, *Yn iach* (good health), which can mean 'goodbye' enforces the uncertainty and sustains the ambiguity in this very lovely elegy (or love poem?). Their relationship was thwarted by:

Clo dur derw, galarchwerw gael,
A daear, deg ei dwyael,
A thromgad ddor, a thrymgae,
A llawr maes rhof a'r lliw mae,
A chlyd fur, a chlo dur du,
A chlicied, yn iach, Lleucu![45]

(A hard oak case, a bitter sad lot, And earth, O fair of feature, And a heavy door, a heavy barrier, A floor of field between her form and me, A sheltering wall, a black steel lock And a latch; goodbye (or fare ye well?) Lleucu![46])

Even when the girl herself proved cooperative, other obstacles could hinder the courtship. Dafydd ap Gwilym describes graphically how difficult it was to develop a satisfactory relat-ionship through 'a small oak window' with its bars and 'row of hindering pillars'.[47] The farm dogs could prove a deterrent and wise suitors would try to remember tasty offerings for the dogs on their night visits. The master or father of the maiden could be obstructive too, although in most cases they claimed ignorance of the secret courting. Poor Dic Coes Bren, from Tregaron, barely escaped with his life when one irate father shot him in the leg while on a courting mission.[48] A major obstacle, quite obviously, could be a jealous husband: for example, the famous *Eiddig* of so many of Dafydd ap Gwilym's poems. Indeed, the challenge of outwitting the *Eiddig*, by indulging in all sorts of horseplay, often assumes more importance in Dafydd's poems than the actual wooing of his mistress.

The young suitor might well, as some of the above descriptions suggest, arrange for an *ysgol garu* (a courtship ladder) to be conveniently located for these night visits. One young woman from Llaniestyn, Llŷn, became so tired of a particular man-servant's visits via the *ysgol garu* that she decided to dig a trench in the garden and bury the ladder forever![49]

Caradoc Evans, whose short stories mercilessly castigate lust and hypocrisy in his interpretation of early twentieth-century Cardiganshire, mentions 'the sound of the gravel on window-pane' several times. Leisa's reaction in 'A Bundle of Life' is typical, for she calls to Abram Bowen, 'You blockhead of a tadpole, is not the old ladder by the pigsty?' and thus he is admitted to her room.[50]

When no *ysgol garu* was available the young lads showed considerable ingenuity, making use of butter churns, pig swill barrels or water pipes as necessary. Innumerable anecdotes have survived of rival suitors interfering with these aids with dire consequences for the innocent party. When Ifan Ffatri Isha went courting Ann Davies, a maid at Mwche farm near Llan-gain, Carmarthenshire Dafydd John, one of the man-servants at the farm, decided to play a trick on him. He sawed through one leg of the butter churn and, when Ifan climbed on to it, it broke under his weight, creating a huge commotion. He had to flee in haste with 'all the dogs of the universe' at his tail. Such horseplay could rebound on the joker. In this case, when Dafydd John the sawyer went courting to Laques farm near Llansteffan, and having gained access to the girl's bedroom, Ifan called by and threw enough stones to 'build a pig-sty' at the Master's bedroom. The whole family awoke and since Dafydd could not leap out of the bedroom window he was forced to make his way in the dark through the farmhouse itself. In his haste he fell headlong into a cauldron full of cream. According to local folk-memory there were three pounds of butter in Dafydd John's pockets when he arrived home at Y Mwche that evening![51] Another aspiring lover suffered the ignominous fate

Courting under the eaves, a lover being hoisted up into the lady's chamber.
(Bibliothèque Nationale)

Courting with the aid of a ladder, the girl garlanding her lover.
(Bibliothèque Nationale)

of falling through the sawn lid of a pig-swill barrel full of the 'most unsavoury mixture'.[52]

One of the strangest accounts of courtship horseplay is found in a ballad by Abel Jones, Y Bardd Crwst, during the second half of the last century. His ballad tells the tale of two young girls who dressed up as lads one May Eve to go courting at a local mansion. They knocked at the window, the girls got up and admitted them at once to their beds—much to the imposters' dismay. The message of the ballad, however, is that women are beginning to throw away their bustles and crinolines and usurp the man's role even in the field of courtship.[53]

With so many obstructions to overcome and hindrances to remove whilst courting 'under the eaves' a young lad would have to be both resourceful and determined to succeed in *mynd i gnocio*. Indeed, the rich vein of poems, rhymes, anecdotes and stories associated with courtship horseplay and the obstacles theme illustrate vividly the wealth of folk-memory and ritual associated with this courtship custom in Wales.

NOTES

[1]D J Williams, *Hen Dŷ Ffarm* (Llandysul, 1954), p.110.
[2]*Cymru,* 1893, p.159.
[3]*Cymru,* 1895, pp.75-6.
[4]W.F.M. Mss 1774.
[5]Stevens, p.14.
[6]*HB,* 462.
[7]J Ceredig Davies, *The Folk-Lore of West and Mid Wales* (Aberystwyth, 1911), p.2; Jenkins, p.125.
[8]Thomas Parry, *Gwaith Dafydd ap Gwilym* (GDG), (Cardiff, 1952), pp.340-2.
[9]Gillis, p.30.
[10]T Gwynn Jones, pp.186-7.
[11]*Llafar Gwlad,* Gaeaf 1985, p.11, Glan Richards.
[12]*Baner ac Amserau Cymru,* Feb. 11, 1880, p.7.
[13]*Cymru,* 1895, pp.75-6.
[14]W H Jones, *Hogyn o Gwm Main* (1985), p.81.
[15]Ibid., p.74.
[16]*HB,* 460.
[17]D Roy Saer, *Caneuon Llafar Gwlad* (WFM, 1974), vol i, 27.
[18]Gillis, pp.28. 122.
[19]Bailey Williams, 'Courtship and Marriage in the late Nineteenth Century in Montgomeryshire,' *Montgomeryshire Collections,* vol. LI, p.120.

[20]E Llwyd Williams, *Crwydro Sir Benfro,* vol.ii, p.55.
[21]W H Jones, p.76.
[22]Rev W Rhys Jones, WFM Ms 2593/63.
[23]Harris, *Country Quest,* 1974, p.36.
[24]Alwyn D Rees, *Life in a Welsh Countryside, A Social Study of Llanfihangel yng Ngwynfa* (Cardiff, 1951), p.84.
[25]*HB,* 465.
[26]Stevens, p.14.
[27]Morris, p.54.
[28]W.F.M. Tape 4858, Mrs J D Roberts, Brynllan, Llanllyfni, A D Rees, p.86.
[29]W.F.M.Tape 4311, John Jones, Pencefnbach, Llannerch-y-medd.
[30]Oral Testimony, J Williams-Davies, W.F.M.
[31]*HB,* 311, 456.
[32]*HB,* 453.
[33]E Llwyd Williams, *Hen Ddwylo* (Llandebie, 1941), pp.19-20; W H Jones, p.76.
[34]Thomas Parry, (edit.), *The Oxford Book of Welsh Verse, (O.B.W.V.),* (Oxford, 1962), 74.
[35]Gwyn Williams, *The Burning Tree* (London, 1956), pp.124-7.
[36]Thomas Roberts, (edit.), *Gwaith Dafydd ab Edmwnd,* (Bangor, 1914), pp.6-8.
[37]Donovan, p.5.
[38]*GDG,* 145.
[39]*HB,* 455.
[40]*HB,* 454.
[41]*HB,* 461.
[42]Ifans, pp.63-5.
[43]W.F.M., Mss 1737/2.
[44]Twm Elias, 'Llen Gwerin', *Llanw Llyn,* Oct. 1984.
[45]*O.B.W.V.*, p.78.
[46]Gwyn Williams, p. 105.
[47]*GDG,* 64, pp.172-3.
[48]W.F.M. Mss 3472/2.
[49]W.F.M. Tape 3112, Ann Williams, Pantycelyn, Llaniestyn, See also Julia Burns 'Yn Wraig i Hen Ffarmwr', *Fferm a Thyddyn* No. 1, 1988, p.6.
[50]Caradoc Evans, *My People* (Severn Books, 1987). p.130.
[51]*Llafar Gwlad,* Gaeaf 1985, p.11.
[52]W H Jones, p.75. See also Atgofion Simon Jones, *Straeon Cwm Cynllwyd* (Gwasg Carreg Gwalch, 1988).
[53]Bangor Mss xxiv, 158.

Chapter 4

'In Stockinged Feet'

The ultimate aim of most of the lovers on their night-visits was to gain entry as soon as possible into the house itself; *cael tŷ.*[1] After spending an appropriate period of time conversing and exchanging pleasantries through the girl's window 'under the eaves' the lad would hope to persuade her to go downstairs and open the door for him. Others, as will be seen later, would climb directly from 'the courtship ladder' into the bedroom itself. Once again, on entering the house, it was essential to be quiet and secretive and the first move the boy would make would be to take off his heavy working shoes and court *yn nhrad 'i sane* (in his stockinged feet). According to an old Pembrokeshire saying *yn nhrad 'i sane ma dewish gwraig*[2] (one should choose one's wife in stockinged feet), while one traditional Welsh verse declared that the only worthy lover was the one who was willing to forget about his shoes:

> Myfi ni charaf yn fy nghalon,
> Ond y pella' ddêl i'm danfon,
> Ac a gerdd yn nhraed ei sanau
> Heb fawr feddwl am ei sgidiau.[3]

(I shall not love in my heart, Any but the furthest who comes to seek me, And who walks in his stockinged feet, Without caring too much about his shoes.)

One rather careless lover from Gwyndy, Anglesey, *c.*1860, took his shoes off, in anticipation, even before climbing up the ladder to the bedroom. Unfortunately, they were discovered by his friends and hidden so that he was forced to walk all the way home in his stockinged feet![4] The same term *yn nhrad 'u sane* (in their stockinged feet), was also applied to two servants from within the same household courting together.[5]

Frequently, the young lads would not arrive until well after dark, about ten or eleven o'clock at night, and, if welcome, they would remain courting in the house until the early hours of the morning. For this reason the custom was called *câl nosweth* (to have a night) or, in south-west Wales, *nosweth o wylad* (a night of watching) (a term also used to describe keeping vigil over a dying or dead person). In Cardiganshire a tired worker would often be railed and provoked, 'he's good for nothing today, he had a night of watching last night'.[6]

If the lad was lucky, the girl would have prepared a fire to keep them warm through the night. In the Llanwrtyd area, Breconshire, a girl was not allowed to burn more than one turf of peat during a courting session and, therefore, the young lads, on peat-cutting days, would try to cut larger and thicker turfs than usual to give to their girlfriends as *mawn caru* (courtship peat) to serve, when needed, during the winter months.[7] Lovers in the Uwchaled area, Denbighshire, would search for wetter pieces of turf than usual as these would burn more slowly and give out heat for a longer period.[8] Home comforts were obviously appreciated:

> Os daw 'nghariad yma heno,
> Mi wna'n ddigon mawr ohono;
> Fe gaiff gadair wellt i eiste'
> Wrth ei glun eisteddaf inne.[9]

(If my loved one comes here tonight, I shall make much of him; He shall have a cane chair to sit on, And I shall sit at his knee.)

Another major attraction to some households was the food prepared for the night visitor(s) and when one recalls the monotonous daily fare of the agricultural labourer this attitude can surely be excused. Edmund Hyde Hall, in his description of Caernarfonshire 1809-11 considered this to be an unworthy motive; '. . . some are stated to be so sadly deficient in sentiment and the higher aspirations of the first of passions, as to mainly select their mistresses with a due regard to the opportunities of their employers' larders'.[10]

Likewise, in Cambridgeshire, the girl's parents would often prepare a light meal for the suitor before they retired for the night, leaving the young pair to court on a big bag of oat chaff and with a blanket or two by the fire.[11] As might be expected, the rhymesters and balladmongers revelled in this aspect of courtship customs, as in this verse from north Pembrokeshire:

Bum yn caru Becca'r Felin,
Lawer nosweth wrth dan eithin;
Ac mi gesim gyda'r himpen
Lawer plated da o boten.[12]

(I have been courting Becca of the Felin, Many nights by the gorse fire; And I had from the wench, Several good platefuls of pudding.)

Pan es i i garu gynta
Mi gefais groesaw mawr;
Ce's foliaid o gaws a thatws,
A stôl i eistedd lawr.

Eilwaith myn'd i garu wedin,
Disgwyl caffael cawl a phwdin;
Beth a gefais gyntaf yno
Gan ei thad ond cael fy nhroedio.[13]

(The first time I went courting, I had a great welcome; I had a bellyful of cheese and potatoes And a stool to sit upon. The second time I went courting, I expected both broth and pudding; The first thing I had there From her father was a kick!)

Two other well-known Welsh ballads feature this aspect of the courting process. In *Y carwr anffodus* (The Unfortunate Lover) we hear of the night visit of Ifan, Tyddyn Fedwen, Llanfihangel, to see Catrin Jane, a local maid-servant. He came straight from his work in the pigsty to the farm and Catrin received him warmly, gave him his fill of *picws mali* (oatcake in butter milk) and then they began courting in earnest, oblivious, it seems, to the stench of pig on Ifan's sleeve. Suddenly, the master and mistress returned, Ifan fled to hide in a cupboard, but the overwhelming smell betrayed him and he was chased from the house 'without his shoes' by the farm dog, Toss. The moral of the story was obvious:

A chofiwch fechgyn annwyl
Ple bynnag byth y bo'ch,
Nad ewch chi byth i garu merch
Yn syth o Gut y moch.[14]

(And remember well, dear boys Wherever you may be, That you should never go courting a girl Straight from the pigsty.)

Couple kissing from the Laws of Hywel Dda.
(National Library of Wales)

The hero of the second ballad found his girlfriend 'with the red hair' rather too generous with her master's fare. He arrived at the house at ten o'clock, knocked gently on the window and, since the family were out, he was admitted to the kitchen. The table was bedecked with delicacies, but he was regaled with more:

A daeth a'r jug â'r brandi,
A'i osod ar y bwrdd,
A d'wedodd, Yfwch cariad,
Y teulu sydd i ffwrdd;
Ac yfed wnes ohono,
Nes gweld ei waelod o,
Ac roeddwn wedi meddwi
A hanner fynd o'm co.

(And she brought the jug with the brandy And placed it on the table, And said Drink, dearest, The family is out; And I drank from it, Until I could see its bottom, And I was drunk And half out of my mind!)

In his drink the young lad became obstreperous, throwing crockery and furniture about. Then suddenly, the master returned and eventually the young lad was arrested for his unruly behaviour. Fortunately, all ended well as he managed to pay his court fine and married his own *hogen goch* (red-haired wench).[15]

There is little other evidence in the Welsh sources of how a courtship would proceed once the lover had gained entry into the kitchen or the *rwm-ford* (table room). Doubtless there was considerable truth in the traditional verse:

Peth ffein yw llaeth a syfi,
Peth ffein yw siwgr candi
Peth ffein yw myned wedi'r nos
I stafell glos i garu.[16]

(Milk and strawberries are nice; Candied sugar is nice,
Going, after nightfall, to a cosy room to court is nice too.)

In order to develop an even more intimate relationship, the Welsh lovers, it seems, would proceed from the kitchen courtship, in the fullness of time, to the bedroom, or they would have entered the bedroom directly via the window and 'courtship ladder' and thus they would *caru'r nos* (court the night); *caru ar y gwely* (court on the bed); or *yn y gwely* (in the bed). This custom was also called *treial criws* (a trial cruise) in the Llandysul area.[17]

Once again, in writing about this stage of courtship, the bards and storytellers loved to emphasize the 'obstacle theme', exploiting to the full the humour of such a situation. Dafydd ap Gwilym, for example, while spending a night at a tavern, attempted to reach 'his mistress's bed' but found his path obstructed by a stool, a table and a cauldron as he struggled to make his way unsuccessfully in the dark. The jerky, stumbling rhythm of this *cywydd* is particularly apt for its theme.[18] The girl herself could prove awkward at the last moment:

Cael yr ysgol ar y pared,
Cael y ffenestr yn agored,
Cael y gwely wedi'i gyweirio
Methu cael f'anwylyd ynddo.[19]

(I got the ladder against the wall, I found the window open, I found the bed prepared, I failed to find my dearest in it.)

As in the ritual of paying court 'under the eaves', rival suitors could try to sabotage the courting; as in the case of the young lad who called upon a maiden at Porth Dinllaen. His rivals waited carefully until he had gained access and then proceeded to create a commotion with the milking pans and pails, awakening the master rudely. And, although the master might have realized the girl was courting and chosen to ignore the fact before the commotion, he had no choice now but to take action. However, this maid-servant was too quick-witted for her master; she took her lover into the buttery and there she found a long bench with the kneading trough alongside it. She made the lad lie on the bench whilst she turned the trough over to hide him, and the master completely failed to find him. He did not even catch the maid, as she knew her way too well around the house.[26]

In most cases, however, the young couple succeeded eventually in reaching the bed and spent the night courting *ar/yn y gwely* (on/in the bed). This custom was probably fairly widely distributed in north-west Europe once, and considerable evidence has survived of its popularity in the Highlands of Scotland, the Western Isles and in Scandinavian countries.[21] We note an interesting paradox in that it was the Puritans who took this custom which they called 'bundling' as they travelled west and settled in North America. Quite a number of books written by travellers to the New World commented upon the prevalence of 'bundling' in North America during the latter part of the eighteenth century. One Connecticut 'greybeard' who was taken to task by his grandson for participating in such a custom replied forthrightly:

> What is the use of sitting up all night and burning out fire and lights, when you could just as well get under kiver and keep warm; and, when you got tired, take a nap and wake up fresh and go at it again?Why d-m it, there wasn't half as many bastards then as there are now!

'Bundling' appears to have died out gradually in North America at the beginning of the nineteenth century.[22] The Americans seem to have become ashamed of this old-world legacy, for when H R Stiles wrote the history of bundling in 1871 his book was kept from the public until 1934 and even then featured in booksellers' terms more as erotica than as social history.[23]

Evidence that the custom existed in England is a little more controversial. In an analysis of Essex court records regarding broken marriage contracts, Alan Macfarlane noted one description of a couple's former relationship, in 1576. According to the witness he had seen the couple:

> lie together alone by the space of two or three hours, her father being at London two or three sundry times, upon one bed in their clothes in the night time in her said father's house, none of them present but this deponent being in bed by them too, of the which this deponent did think no offence for that they minded to marry together.[24]

Yet this author denies quite categorically that 'bundling' which he defines as fertility-testing ever existed in England:

> No foreign observer, no moralist castigating the sexual behaviour of the lower orders, no individual defending his or her behaviour against the church authorities, no diarist or autobiographer describing his courtship, speaks of the need to be sure that a partner could bear children before the couple could marry.[25]

Likewise, Quaife in his detailed study of *Wanton Wenches and Wayward Wives* based on depositions between 1601 and 1660 to Quarter Sessions in the County of Somerset to the Consistory Courts of the Diocese of Bath and Wells, states quite categorically that 'Bundling . . . seems to be absent in the West Country. No trace of it emerged in the court records'.[26]

The confusion arises because 'bundling' in fact was not synonymous with fertility testing; it had a wider, more innocent meaning as in '*caru ar y gwely*'. There is certainly evidence that in this latter meaning the custom was known in England, especially in regions such as Cheshire and Cornwall in close contact with Wales. It was the migrant Irish labour force which popularized the custom amongst the Fen villages of Littleport, East Anglia.[27] It should also be noted that Thomas Hardy, in his novel *The Well-Beloved*, which was located on the Isle of Slingers, or

Portland, near Weymouth, makes use of what he claims to be an old island custom of proving fertility by trial marriage as a very important element in the development of his plot.[28]

There can be little doubt of the popularity and prevalence of the custom in Wales, although Welsh authors and poets have not dwelt unduly on *caru yn y gwely*. It was treated as a totally natural, ordinary occurrence which did not merit undue attention. Giraldus Cambrensis, the tireless medieval traveller and inspired chronicler, was the first to mention the custom, as far as is known, in his *Description of Wales*, 1194.[29] Giraldus, in fact, was the only Welsh commentator to associate the custom with any kind of fertility test or trial marriage. Later in the Middle Ages Dafydd ap Gwilym, as one might expect, exploited the possibilities of such a mode of courtship to the full in his poetry. In a poem denying that he had ever been a monk, he reminds his fair one:

Aethost, wi o'r gost a'r gamp,
I'th wely, bryd wyth wiwlamp,
A'th freichiau, hoen blodau haf
Em y dynion, amdanaf.[30]

(*You went*, alas the cost and the feat, *To your bed*, the beauty of eight radiant lights, *With your arms*, the colour of summer flowers, Men's gem, *around me*.)

Of all life's pleasures, Dafydd's favourites were:

Cydfod mwyn, cydyfed medd,
Cydarwain, serch, cydorwedd.[31]

(Being together tenderly, drinking mead together, Making love together, lying together.)

As *cydorwedd* (lying together) was the accepted norm for lovers in Wales during Dafydd's period, one can therefore appreciate that what might seem to be the poet's constant boasting about his manly prowess merely reflects the situation of a lover in the Middle Ages.

Some of the best descriptions of the custom in Wales, albeit much later, emanate however, not from Welsh sources, but from the writings of the numerous romantic travellers who visited Wales towards the end of the eighteenth and early nineteenth centuries. They were fascinated to observe some of the quaint customs of what they considered to be the rather uncivilized Welsh peasantry; and since *caru ar y gwely* had obviously become more or less obsolete in England, the English travellers revelled in exploring and describing the custom in Wales. One of the first to venture into this field was J Jackson, who visited Merionethshire in 1772 and who strove to capture the essence of *caru ar y gwely* in his writings, despite his own considerable shortcomings for the work:

> Here the nymphs receive their admirers in bed. The circumstance is notorious, yet common as it is, it is a difficult matter especially by one that is married and an Englishman to ascertain with any appearance of credibility.

Yet by accident, he was fortunate enough to catch a glimpse of the custom one Saturday night, when a nearby farmer's son came visiting the girl in the farmhouse where he was staying:

> To assist my narrative on this occasion I shall call the principal personages of the drama, Colin and Phebe. The latter had taken off her head-dress and was adjusting her hair . . . She then very deliberately pulled off and folded up her outer garments, . . . keeping on only a short coat over her chammese, the tucker of which she carefully drew very close about her neck. Colin, all this time, with everything on but his hat and shoes, was standing near the head of the bed . . . The affairs of her homely toilet at length being adjusted she took the candle in her hand. Colin sat upon the bed. Phebe went round and got in on the farther side. The crimson of her cheek brightened as she gave her lover a last look for the evening and, putting out the light, left me and yourself to form our own conclusion from the foregoing transaction.

And although his observations were quite naturally curtailed, Jackson's further impressions of the scene are worth noting:

> During this whole progress I must confess there were such striking marks exhibited of innate virtue as entirely expunged from my mind every disadvantageous prejudice lodged there by the repeated accounts I had heard of a Welsh courtship. And I am

thoroughly convinced that the conversation which afterwards succeeded betwixt the young couple was as truly modest as the dumb show of the candle-light scene had been unexceptionally innocent.[32]

Twenty-five years later, another traveller, a Mr Pratt, visited Wales and took a special interest in this matter. He had obviously been forewarned that courting in the bed was common practice amongst the 'lower order of people', therefore:

> . . . I really took some pains to investigate this curious custom, and after being assured, by many, of its veracity, had an opportunity of attesting its existence with my own eyes. The servant-maid of the family I visited in Caernarvonshire, happened to be the object of a young peasant, who walked eleven long miles every Sunday morning, to savour his suit, and regularly returned the same night through all weathers, to be ready for Monday's employment . . . He usually arrived in time for morning service . . . after which he escorted his Dulcinea home to the house of her master, by whose permission they as constantly passed the succeeding hour in bed, according to the custom of the country.

This is the only description that has survived in Wales which suggests that *caru ar y gwely* went on in the daytime, even on a Sunday, and yet there is no reason to doubt the evidence. According to Pratt, this relationship continued for two years before the couple entered into matrimony and all that while the situation was not abused. He concludes, therefore, that the custom must be as innocent as any other:

> One proof of it being thought so by the parties is the perfect ease and freedom with which it is done, no awkwardness or confusion appearing on either side; the most well-behaved and decent young women giving in to it without a blush . . . The power of habit is, perhaps, stronger than the power of passion . . . and it is sufficient, almost, to say a thing is the custom of the country to clear it from any reproach that would attach to an innovation.[33]

Another traveller, J T Barber, on his tour of north Wales and Monmouthshire in 1803[34] merely noted the custom in passing, while the Reverend W Bingley in 1804 dwelt more fully upon the subject.[35] He also associated the custom with the 'peasantry' of the three northern counties of Caernarvonshire, Anglesey and Merionethshire and described the lover stealing, under the shadow of night, to his fair one's room. He noted that the lover retained 'an essential part of his dress' but the Reverend reserved judgement as to the innocence of the custom, fearing that the true consequences would not be fully revealed until two or three months after the marriage ceremony.

No such doubts troubled the mind of another visitor to Wales in 1856. Julius Rodenberg seems to have been an impossible romantic and his description of the custom is fanciful if not inaccurate. He observed courting the night at Wern, Llanfairfechan,where the daughter of the household, Sarah, was being visited by Owen, her beau:

> I heard only a sound which indicated that Owen was taking off his boots and Sarah her shoes. And truly—in stockinged feet they came up the stairs, past my chamber and into Sarah's little room opposite.

Rodenberg turned to the local schoolmaster for an explanation which heartened him greatly:

> the girl sits on her bed chatting with her beloved until the morning. But don't believe that anything unseemly happens; the girl . . . would flee in terror from the lover who abused this opportunity—indeed, he would have to think himself lucky if he got away without a bloody nose. In a few days the news of his shamelessness would reach the ear of every girl in the neighbourhood, his friends would avoid him with loathing and his job, his happiness, indeed, his whole future would be seriously jeopardised.[36]

In general, however, there was a reluctance to depend wholly upon the girl's moral character and efforts were usually made to protect the girl's chastity and virginity.

In Cape Cod, Connecticut, in 1827, the girl would put on:

> a very appropriate and secure nightdress, made neither like a bloomer or mantilla, but something like a common dress, excepting the lower part, which is furnished with legs, like drawers properly attached. The dress is drawn at the neck and waist with strings tied with a very strong knot, and over this is put the ordinary apparel.[37]

Similarly, in Wales, in the Cerrigydrudion area, a large stocking would be on hand. The girl would be tied to her waist in this to prevent her coming to any harm while courting in the night.[38] References have also been found to arming the girl with a lethal hat pin, whilst placing a large bolster down the centre of the bed could prove to be a useful deterrent. Indeed, a saying has derived from the custom of using a bolster in this manner in order to denigrate a man who is not as much of a Romeo as he claims to be, *Hy, doedd e ddim yn gallu jwmpo dros ben bolster!* (Hm, he couldn't even jump over a bolster!) The bolster was the safeguard recommended in the novel *The Black Venus* by Rhys Davies, which discussed in detail the merits and demerits of *caru ar y gwely*. In this novel, published in 1944, but describing Edwardian Wales and located in Ayron, an imaginary village in south-west Wales, the heroine, Olwen, heiress of Tŷ Rhosyn, is tried by the village elders for engaging in the age-long custom of courting in bed. The vicar, egged on by an English divorcee, wished to see the practice abolished while the majority of the villagers, including the nonconformist minister, who had themselves courted on the bed in their youth, failed to see why the custom should be changed. The ritual had been used in the past 'to prove if the woman would rise like a good loaf of bread' and one witness in the trial testified that in his grandfather's time in Merionethshire it had been customary, 'to stitch the courters up in a sack for all night, a sack special made to fit two, close and tidy. Stitched up fast they were inside by parents of the woman and left all night on the bed'. Although this practice had been discontinued according to the novel, the heroine defended the custom itself as a means of educating young men in the techniques of chivalrous courtship, and because it allowed couples to become thoroughly acquainted, though not carnally, before venturing into marriage. The judge in the trial concluded that the custom should be continued and that the best protection for the young girl would be a 'well-stuffed and full-length bolster'.[39]

The girl was not always the innocent, defenceless victim, as the author of this ballad collected in the Llandysul area *c.*1900-25, found to his dismay:

Mi drawodd ar fy meddwl Ac hefyd ar fy serch
I fyned ar ryw noswaith i fferm i dreio'r ferch,
Ffal di ral . . .

Mi gnociais yn y ffenest, lle roedd y ddau liw rhos
Atebai'r ferch yn union . . . 'Mae'n llawer iawn o'r nos,

Dewch yma nos yfory Rhyw awr neu ddwy ynghynt
Cewch ddod gen i i'r gwely O dan y bing a'r quilt'.

Mi droiais innau'n nghefen Gan feddwl myned bant
Ond gwaeddai'r feinwen fwynaidd, 'O ewch i ddrws y ffront'

Ces ganddi fynd i'r gwely Beth fynswn gael yn well?
Ond pe bawn i ond gwybod, Mi redswn bant ym mhell . . .

Mi gydiodd am fy nghanol, Gan ddweyd 'O fanwyl ffrynd
Os mentrwch i'r fan hyny Mae croeso i chi fynd.'

Pe bawn i ddim ond gwybod Na ddoi un mab i'r byd
Mi awn o fodd fy nghalon, I glatsho'r boliau 'nghyd.[40]

(It struck my mind And also my desire To go one evening to a farm to try the girl, Ffal di ral . . . I knocked on the window, where the rose coloured one was The girl answered immediately 'It's very late in the night, Come back tomorrow night An hour or two earlier. You can come to bed with me under the bing [coverlet?] and the quilt'. I turned my back Intending to go away But the sweet girl was shouting, 'O come to the front door'. I got her to go to bed What more could I ask? If I had only known I would have run far away. She grabbed my waist, Saying 'O dear friend If you venture that far, You're welcome to go even further'. If I could only know That no son would come into the world I would be delighted to go there, and to clap the stomachs together.)

Such forward girls would, no doubt, seek the advice of the older generation on contraceptive potions. If they lived in the Ffair-rhos area of Cardiganshire one of the old wives might have recited the following lines:

Ceisiwch afu dwy lysywen
A dwy lleden yn y glyn,
Swigen penwhigyn, afu morgrugyn,

Deunaw ewyn y greinyn gwyn;
Afu malwod, llath y llygod,
Bloneg draenog, sgyfen dryw,
Hyn a geidw'r eneth ifanc
Rhag beichiogi tra bo'i byw.[41]

(Seek the liver of two eels. And two plaice in the glen, herring's bladder, an ant's liver, eighteen nails of the white toad [?] Snail's livers, mice's milk, a hedgehog's fat, a wren's lung, This will keep the young girl from conceiving as long as she lives.)

The extract of the Talgarreg version which has survived is even less respectable:

Hadel y bolie gwynion godi
Hadel y bronne lanw o lath . . .
Esgyrn llygod, danne malwod,
Bloneg draenog, ceille dryw . . .[42]

(To prevent the white stomachs rising, To prevent the breasts filling with milk . . . Mice bones, snails' teeth, hedgehog fat, and wren's testicles . . .)

These are obviously nonsense verses or witches' potions but perhaps the girl could be discouraged from going too far by the prospect of such an antidote to pregnancy.

Although the exact details of the custom of *caru ar y gwely* varied from period to period, from place to place and obviously from couple to couple, certain elements remained constant. There can be little doubt that the parents or employers were well aware of its existence and they probably condoned it without obviously encouraging it. An early nineteenth-century doctor, who knew his Cardiganshire patients very well, described them courting 'on the beds . . . in the sight and with the approbation of their mutual friends and relations'.[43] Likewise, in the *Report of the Commission to inquire into the Poor Law,* 1834 it was admitted that the custom was so powerful 'that many gentlemen state that they must either overlook the fact of their female servants giving in to it or, make up their minds to employ only men servants or old women.'[44] According to an informant in the Trawsfynydd (Merioneth) area, as part payment for his services and to celebrate the end of the hay harvest, a man-servant would be allowed to court on the bed with the maid-servant of his choice[45].

Courting on the bed could continue for several years as some of the above references indicate. One of the few written Welsh accounts of the custom and which comes from the Llandysul area, illustrates this further:

> I was sixteen years old when I began courting in bed with my Mari fach . . . We courted in bed for two years, every Saturday night. I don't know how others feel, but I felt that there was nothing more heavenly than being in her arms, and in the morning she could be found sleeping in my arms, that we had no reason to be ashamed of the previous night.[46]

Such exemplary behaviour! Sometimes the lover protests his innocence rather too loudly. Hywel Dafi, a poet from Gwent (*c.* 1450-80) describes bundling as the 'love of innocent young children' for:

> We lay naked side by side
> suffering the same pain nightly
> without intending, my slender darling
> sin any more than children . . .[47]

The poem is entitled, suggestively enough, 'Frustration'!

Courting could, and often would, continue into the early hours and even into break of day. In one *cywydd* the intrepid Dafydd ap Gwilym vents his anger against the dawn for breaking so early and interrupting his lovemaking.[48]

Another lover, one Dafydd Wynn, the hero of a poem by Bardd Nantglyn, took adequate precautions against sleeping too late after courting on the bed. He decided to take his cockerel a-courting with him

> *Fel byddai'r bore'n barod,*
> *Rhag cysgu'n hynod hir,*
> *Fe'i rhoe ar ben y gwely,*
> *I ganu, a dweyd y gwir.*

(So that he would be ready in the morning,In case he slept too long, He'd put him at the head of the bed, To sing, to tell the truth.)

Unfortunately, however, our hero forgot to take other, perhaps more important, precautions:

Peth difyr iawn wrth garu,
Yw tynu at y crys,
Ca'dd Dafydd Wynn am hynny
Roi'r fodrwy wrth ei fys.[49]

(It's a very pleasant thing while courting to undress down to the shirt, For that Dafydd Wynn had to Put a ring around his finger.)

Long hours and persistent night-visiting could adversely affect a young lad's performance at work:

> many young men 'sit up' three or four nights a week, each with a different girl and they can scarcely be expected to be such efficient workmen in the days that follow.[50]

Stringent efforts were continuously made to explain and excuse the old custom of 'courting in/on the bed' especially by visitors to Wales who did not wish to be accused of treating the natives unfairly. Certainly Jackson took some pains to justify its origin:

> The houses of the Old Britons were not supplied with a variety of apartments, a common room to sit in, another for the beds of the family, being all the accommodation that most of them could boast of. Courtship to a young couple was not very agreeable amidst the jests of a crowded fireside, stolen meetings to lovers being always most pleasing. The weather amongst the mountains is frequently wet . . . The bedroom was therefore the most obvious place of retirement. Candles were not perhaps always allowed . . . To sit in darkness on the side of the bed was therefore most eligible. The young folks were often wearied . . . to lie down during their innocent chat was most easy, and disabled them the less from pursuing the labours of the following day.[51]

This very practical interpretation of the practice was echoed by others. D J Williams emphasized the hard labour of the farm-servant and the difficulties of courting on a chair, a bench, or cushionless settle in front of the fire[52] while the *Commission of Inquiry into the State of Education in Wales*, in 1847, drew frequent attention to the squalid and inadequate housing of the Welsh peasantry. Cottages in the Tal-y-llyn area, Merionethshire, comprised, they claimed, of 'one room in which all the family sleep' and comments such as 'sleeping, accommodation unsatisfactory', 'lamentable deficiency of bedroom accommodation' and 'the gravest evil is the want of bedroom accommodation' occur time after time in the Commissioners' Blue Books.[53] Doubtless, the long hours farm-servants worked contributed to the practical attraction of the custom. A tale from the Llanwrtyd area illustrates the interminable nature of a maid-servant's duties. A young lad had gone to look for his girlfriend to arrange a night yn *caru ar y gwely*. She replied that she would be quite prepared to court the night with him once her farm duties had been completed correctly:

Ar ôl llwydo dŵr afonydd
Troi coed â'u bonau fynydd,
A thynnu'r marw dros y byw,
Dof atat, Huw, yn ufudd.[54]

(After dirtying the river water [washing the dishes] Turning the logs upside down And covering the fire with small coal I shall come to you obediently, Huw.)

These comments would seem to place the old custom of courting on the bed in perspective and in its true social context. Easy for us today to mock this quaint and romantic custom. We must not forget that living conditions among the working and labouring classes throughout the centuries were notoriously inadequate. People, other than the yeomanry and landed gentry, lived in poverty, squalor and stench; for them there was little hope of escaping their social imprisonment. If courting the night could, therefore, alleviate somewhat this grim regime, it is hardly surprising that the young people indulged so frequently and enthusiastically in *caru ar y gwely*.

NOTES

[1]D J Williams, p.110.
[2]Morris, p.100.
[3]*HB*, 480.
[4]Oral testimony, William Evans, Corwen, 1985.
[5]W H Jones, p.74.
[6]Jenkins, p.126.
[7]W.F.M., Mss 1793/309, Evan Jones, Tynypant, Llanwrtyd.
[8]W.F.M. Tape 1360, Lewis T Evans, Seler, Cyfylliog.
[9]*HB*, 458.
[10]Edmund Hyde Hall, *A Description of Caernarvonshire, (1809-1811)* (Caernarvon, 1952), p.323.
[11]Enid Porter, *Cambridgeshire Customs and Folklore* (London, 1969), p.4.
[12]Morris, p.164.
[13]*Bye-gones,* 1 Dec., 1897, W.F.M. Tape 4610, Owen Hughes, Hendre Bach, Cerrigydrudion.
[14]W.F.M. Mss 1420, Lewis T Evans, Seler, Cyffylliog.
[15]*Cerddi Cymru,* 20.
[16]*Cyfaill yr Aelwyd,* March 1883, p.174.
[17]Oral testimony, Mrs Hanna Jones, Llandysul, 1984.
[18]*Welsh Verse,* translations by Tony Conran, (Poetry Wales Press, 1986), pp.174-6.
[19]*HB*, 457.
[20]Catrin Parri Huws, *Sul Gŵyl a Gwaith* (Gwasg Gwynedd, 1981), p.82.
[21]*By Og Bygd,* Nork FolkeMuseums Arbok, 1948-49, p.59; *Fataburen,* 1969, pp.25-52.
[22]W John Rowe, 'Old World Legacies in America', *Folk Life*, Vol. 6, p.73.
[23]Henry Reed Stiles, *Bundling, Its Origins, Progress and Decline in America* (First edit, 1871, New York 1934), publisher's note.
[24]Macfarlane, p.298.
[25]Ibid., p.306.
[26]G R Quaife, *Wanton Wenches and Wayward Wives,* (London, 1979), p.247.
[27]Porter, Cambridgeshire Customs . . . p.3,5; quoting a song about bundling sung in the tap room at the Ship Inn at Brandon Creek.
[28]Thomas Hardy, *The Well-Beloved* (London, 1975), p.40; See further Gillis, pp. 126-7.
[29]Thomas Jones, 'Gerald the Welshman's "Itinerary through Wales" and "Description of Wales",' *National Library of Wales Journal,* Vol. vi, 1949-50, p.214.
[30]*GDG,* 35.
[31]Ibid., 74.
[32]J Jackson, 'Letters from and Relating to North Wales, *Transactions of the Merionethshire Historical Society,* vol.v, 1965-8, pp. 212-3.
[33]Mr Pratt, *Gleanings through Wales, Holland and Wesphalia* (London, 1797) vol.i, pp. 105-7.
[34]J T Barber, *A Tour throughout North Wales and Monmouthshire,* (1803).
[35]Rev W Bingley, *North Wales; Including its Scenery, Antiquities and Customs* (London, 1804), vol.ii, p.282.
[36]Julius Rodenberg, *An Autumn in Wales (1856),* (translated and edited by William Linnard, 1985), p.29.
[37]Stiles, p. 113.
[38]W.F.M. Tape 4611, Owen Hughes, Hendre Bach, Cerrigydrudion.
[39]Rhys Davies, *The Black Venus* (Heinemann Ltd. 1944).
[40]W.F.M. Mss. 1737/1-6, J Ffos Davies, Blaenffos.

[41]Oral testimony, Mary Jones, Ffair-rhos, Cardiganshire.

[42]W.F.M. Mss 2181/98, W Beynon Davies, Bron Hendre, Y Waun Fawr, Aberystwyth.

[43]E W Jones, 'Medical Glimpses of Early Nineteenth Century Cardiganshire.', *National Library of Wales Journal,* vol.xiv, (1965-6), pp.260-75.

[44]*Report of the Major Commission to Inquire into the Poor Law, 1834,* Appendix A, p.180.

[45]W.F.M. Tape 4611, Owen Hughes, Hendre Bach, Cerrigydrudion.

[46]W J Davies, p.280.

[47]D Johnston, *Canu Maswedd yr Oesoedd Canol, Medieval Welsh Erotic Poetry,* (Cardiff, 1991), p.63.

[48]*GDG,* 129.

[49]W.F.M. Mss 1905/7.

[50]*Royal Commission on Labour,* p.63.

[51]J Jackson, p.213.

[52]D J Williams, p.111.

[53]I C Peate, *The Welsh House* (1940), pp.88,93.

[54]W.F.M. Mss 1793/51.

Chapter 5

The Chastity Movement

The custom of 'courting the night' may have been totally acceptable and extremely practical in the opinion of the early Romantic tourists to Wales but it was also, and most importantly, the accepted practice amongst the mass of the Welsh populance until about 1800. Yet, barely a century and a quarter later it had almost disappeared from the countryside. The reasons for this are complex and often relate indirectly to the changing of the very fabric of rural society; to increasing urbanization and its impact; to the sense of inferiority which plagued the Welsh after the prejudiced and unfavourable reports on the morality of the Welsh people in the 1847 *Commission of Inquiry into the State of Education in Wales*, known as 'The Treason of the Blue Books', and to many other interrelated social, economic and psychological factors. All these facets must be borne in mind in any treatment and analysis of courting customs in nineteenth-century Wales. However, there was also a concerted effort, which amounted almost to a campaign, to reform the courting rituals of the young and to rid the country of the supposed immorality of *caru ar y gwely*.

In America, these sentiments were expressed in some of the early nineteenth-century ballads, depicting those who upheld the custom as hopeless sinners:

> Deep down in hell, there let them dwell
> And bundle on that bed,
> Then turn and roll without control
> Till all their lusts are fed.[1]

While their Welsh counterparts were not as severely censured, the disgrace and futility of the custom was again emphasized in verse:

> *Poen wrth garu, poen wrth beidio,*
> *Poen wrth droi fy nghariad heibio,*
> *Poen wrth godi'r nos i'r ffenest*
> *Gwell yw byw yn eneth onest.*[2]

(Pain from courting, pain from not courting, Pain from turning my loved one away, Pain from getting up to the window at night. It is best to live as an honest wench.)

The reforming campaign was mounted on several fronts and found supporters in various social circles and religious denominations. Some chose to dissuade the sons and daughters of farmers from engaging in *caru ar y gwely* by arguing that it was a custom fit only for the 'lower order of people', for the poorer labouring classes. According to the testimony of the witnesses before the *Commission on Labour, The Agricultural Labourer,* in 1893, this argument had proven to be a powerful one, for in his Report, D Lleufer Thomas commented thus on 'bundling':

> These customs are not so prevalent as they were nearly 50 years ago. The chief difference perhaps is that at present these practices are mainly, but by no means exclusively, confined to the labouring class, while at an earlier date it was the ordinary mode of courtship with the sons and daughters of farmers and the younger members of the rural population generally.[3]

The vivid descriptions of the custom in the works of the early travellers to Wales made the Welsh people suddenly aware that *caru ar y gwely* had long since disappeared from what they regarded as superior, sophisticated English society and that although it was perhaps 'quaint' it was also considered to be primitive and unacceptable to modern society. This was one of the main arguments peddled in the denominational literature of the period, such as in *Y Dysgedydd*, 1834:

> . . . in which place, in which country, do lads and lasses meet together in the hay lofts, in the barns, and go to secret places, far away, out of men's hearing, to fulfil their illicit love . . . to bring disgrace upon themselves, upon their relatives, upon the area in which they live, upon the country in which they reside and upon the nation to which they belong?[4]

This particular criticism of the old Welsh custom was echoed forty years later in a newspaper article:

> We are the butt of the Englishman's derision and contempt because of this custom.[5]

The primitive nature of the custom was emphasized, and mocked, time after time, in the 1847 *Commission of Inquiry into the State of Education in Wales*. Although many of the findings and comments in the Report were accurate and to prove valuable for historians, the Commissioners decided not to confine their brief to education but rather to launch into a virulent attack upon the moral character of the Welsh people. They claimed that most of the immorality stemmed directly from the continued existence of courting the night in Wales and based their conclusions upon the testimony of such witnesses as the Reverend J Pugh, Vicar of Llandeilo Fawr:

> The state of morals among the labouring population is bad; habitual lying and low cunning are very commonly met with, and unchastity is so prevalent that great numbers of the young women are in the family-way previous to marriage; and this sin, I fear, is very lightly regarded.

Thus the Commissioner could conclude of Dewisland Hundred in Pembrokeshire that, as a result of the prevalence of bundling:

> I heard the most revolting anecdotes of the gross and almost bestial indelicacy with which sexual intercourse takes place on these occasions. In the parochial notes . . . the moral character of the population is generally returned by the clergy and others as good . . . the common acceptation of the words *good character* to be the absence of legal rather than moral offences.[6]

As with hiring fairs, sterling efforts were made by the reformers to link bundling directly with a high illegitimacy rate in rural Wales. Certainly this was the opinion of several of those who appeared before the *Commission on the Employment of Children, Young Persons and Women in Agriculture* in 1867. The Reverend William Owen, a Baptist minister, felt confident that:

> with the custom of fathers domiciling the male servants in out-houses, . . . whence they prowl about in the night . . . seeking and obtaining intercourse with the girls through the night, arise the many cases of bastardy which we hear in the county.

Mr William Phillips of Arberth reluctantly agreed that this correlation was relevant:

> The rate of bastardy is, I believe, on the decrease; the cause of its being at the present rate is the great levity allowed to farm servants in spending nights together courting.[7]

Certainly the statistics provided in the Annual Reports of the Registrar General of Births, Marriages and Deaths do seem to indicate that illegitimacy rates were higher in rural areas (in the areas where courting the night was most common) and this pattern is in marked contrast with the European pattern of higher urban illegitimacy. Between 1893 and 1910, the illegitimacy ratio for Wales averages 3.41 per 1000 births while the averages for rural Welsh-speaking Cardiganshire was 5.64; for industrial Glamorganshire 2.69. Further analysis confirms this rural lead, for within Carmarthenshire between 1885 and 1909 the illegitimacy ratio of rural Cynwyl Gaeo was 8.89; Llanfihangel-ar-Arth 7.34 and Llanelli Urban District 2.29. (Again, all figures are per 1000 births.)[8]

It was the hypocrisy which sought to deny and conceal this rural immorality which so inflamed the author Caradoc Evans, for according to his interpretation of the custom, every instance of courting in bed, resulted in unwanted pregnancy. In 'Greater than Love', Esther accuses her lover, Sam, of having another relationship which has already gone too far, for she asks,

> 'Is there not loud speakings that you have courted Catrin in bed? Very full is her belly.'[9]

This theme is repeated in many of his other short stories.

There can be no doubt that in many, if not most, cases of such free behaviour, the young girls had been seduced to succumb to their lovers by promises of betrothal; as befitted girls brought up in a society which placed such a high value upon virginity, chastity and marriage. In Carmarthenshire, fifty percent of illegitimate births were the result of a promise of betrothal. One Margaret Jones of Mill Terrace, Pantyffynnon, Ammanford, for example, had courted in bed with John Bowen, a collier, under parental supervision for three years, before she succumbed and was then abandoned.[10] Under such circumstances, family and social pressures could be brought to bear to force the young men to wed the girls and thus the offspring would be considered legitimate.

Even when the young lover could not be prevailed upon to honour his promise, private agreements could be made for maintenance of the child, without resource to magisterial decision. These children would often be brought up by the parents of the pregnant girl as their own legitimate offspring. To avoid scandal, some pregnant girls might be sent away until the time of delivery and then return home with a new member for her own family. A large number of Somerset girls, it seems, during the seventeenth century, awaited the delivery of their illegitimate children in Wales. According to Quaife, those from east Somerset travelled through Gloucester into Monmouth and those from the west were trans-shipped from Minehead to a variety of Welsh ports, usually in Glamorgan, for 'Wales was the popular haven'.[11] Other young mothers, in spite of great hardship and poverty, succeeded in maintaining their children themselves. A considerable number of conceptions also miscarried, the child might be stillborn or might die in childbirth.

However, before the beginning of the nineteenth century those young mothers who could not support themselves and their children were considered to present a major problem for their community and especially for their parish. The parish did everything it could to keep pregnant girls on the move for it could ultimately be held responsible for the maintenance of the mother and child if all else failed. A pregnant mother could be hounded back, at great physical risk, to the parish of her birth but again these parishioners would not wish to be forced to maintain her illegitimate offspring as well. The girl would be coerced to reveal the father's name in a bastardy order. A quarter of those subject to such an order would also have to suffer the ignominious fate of being whipped in public on market day at the local market town. One Agnes Poole, of Norton Fitzwarren, was to be taken in 1621, 'on Sunday next . . . immediately after evening prayers to be whipped severely through the streets of the parish until her body be bloody'. Others would be placed in the House of Correction and privately whipped.[12]

The Poor Law Amendment Act of 1834 made the position of the pregnant spinster even more difficult. Under the terms of this act it became easier for the supposed father to evade or defy the law. He could no longer be imprisoned and thus was exempted from payment in person when he could, or would, not pay in purse. A further act of 1844 forced uneducated girls to try to make claims for maintenance in open court, without any help from the Poor Law Guardians. In 1891 three or four cases of affiliation a week would come before the Caernarfonshire courts[13] and between 1900-14 there were as many as 756 cases in Carmarthenshire alone.[14] These Affiliation Orders, Reports and Transcripts 'reveal the savage personal tragedies which lie concealed beneath the superficially placid facades of social institutions'.[15]

The mother had to corroborate allegations of paternity if she wished to serve an 'Affiliation Order' on the alleged father. A servant girl, sexually abused by a social superior, stood little chance before the court and often the girl would be dismissed as a scheming temptress or experienced slut. Sarah Jenkins, a thirty-year-old servant from Bryn, Llanelli, was portrayed as a 'scheming corrupter of youth' in her paternity case against Edgar Thomas, the twenty-two-year-old son of her employer; while Edith May Williams of the 'Plough and Harrow', Glanaman, found that her work as a barmaid prejudiced the hearing against her, although she could call upon four witnesses to testify to her relationship with the defendant.[16] For many girls the attempt to portray themselves as the innocent party resulted in a series of character assassinations and moral onslaughts from the defendant's lawyer and witnesses. Many young women were extremely reluctant to subject themselves to such a degrading experience.

It is hardly surprising, therefore, that pregnant girls sought other solutions for their problems. The most common was abortion either by physical exertion 'to bruise her body thereby to destroy the child'[17] or through potions of a medicinal nature and administered orally. Newspapers carried thinly disguised advertisements for abortifacients such as 'The Magic Female Pills' and 'Lady Heseldine's Female Corrective Mixture'. Even the sober Welsh-language paper of the Independent denomintion *Y Tyst*, carried advertisements such as these for their female clientele. Tragically, these potions, and other methods of abortion, often went seriously wrong and many young girls suffered cruelly, both mentally and physically, as a result.[18]

If such methods failed, and the child was born, the young mother, unable to maintain it herself, and with no other support, would have to make a desperate choice. The baby could be farmed out, at a cost, to a baby farmer, usually an older woman or couple. Although this could be viewed as a humanitarian solution, in most cases the baby farmers themselves would be desperately poor and the child would invariably be neglected and exploited. The alternative would be to abandon the baby or even to conceal its birth. This crime was the second most common offence, after petty theft, committed by women in rural areas during the nineteenth century. According to a study of rural Pembrokeshire gaol records, of a total of 214 cases brought before the courts between 1800 and 1891 forty-one or nineteen percent were charges concerning the concealment of the births and deaths of children.[19] If the defendant was found guilty she could be sentenced to capital punishment. Indeed, infanticide peaked in 1860 and one comes across many horrific descriptions of discovering rotting infant corpses in mines, drains, quarries and woodlands during the Victorian era.

It is difficult and probably impossible to prove that these tragic aspects of rural life, the illegitimacies, the abortions, the concealments of births and so forth can be directly related and attributed to the Welsh custom of courting on the bed. Yet any study of the lighter aspects of the custom, with its mischievous horseplay and element of harmless fun, which feature so vividly in folk memory, must be balanced carefully against the sobering tales of the cruel reality of rural nineteenth-century Wales.

All these different factors and arguments contributed in various degrees to the numerous campaigns mounted to eliminate *caru ar y gwely* as a Welsh courting custom. The denominational periodicals were the first into the fray with lively and highly-coloured descriptions of the effects of pursuing the custom. *Seren Gomer*, in 1818, drew the readers' attention to the:

> immoral unchastity which is thriving and to implore Ministers of Religion and religious figures to devote themselves to destroying the great and evil blemish.[20]

While a correspondent to the *Eurgrawn Wesleyaidd* in 1819 felt that stronger language was needed:

> the majority of Gomer's sons, especially of the lower order, love to make prostitutes of their wives before marrying them; . . . O my God, what would idol worshippers and all Christianity's enemies say if they heard that prostitution thrives best in the areas where there are most sermons and religious persons . . . I understand—that some argue boldly of the innocence of courting through the night,—two or three nights a week—and that over a period of years, in the bed! . . . Suffice it for me to show that such a custom is unseemly,—leads naturally to vulgarity, gives succour to immorality, and is a disgrace to any civilised nation on earth.[21]

The campaign gathered momentum gradually with the century and became reinforced by the parallel efforts of the temperance movement which swept through Britain in the thirties and forties. In 1840 the Methodists of Dolgellau decided that it was time to form an anti-bundling society and in their first meeting called upon all the chapel's congregation to sign a pledge to abstain from courting in bed. Seventeen of the men agreed to do so, though they were all, ironically, well over forty years old. The girls refused to conform until all the young men in the area had signed first; and the society failed at its outset.[22] A similar society, called 'The Chastity Society to prevent degrading intercourse amongst the nation' was formed at Pentrellyncymer, Denbighshire in the same year and the rules of membership were detailed in *Y Dysgedydd*:

> Let not the lads charm and tempt girls to associate furtively at this time . . . Let not the girls agree, if they are tempted . . . Let not the parents and heads of households allow such dangerous disorder in their houses . . . We approve of association by letter writing, and short visits, at suitable times and in suitable places.[23]

The society formed at Aber-banc, Henllan, Cardiganshire in 1850 was fired by the same motivation. The first meeting of the society 'to abolish bad morals and unchastity' was chaired by T D Lloyd, the local squire, and he was ably assisted by a host of local clergy and ministers. In the meeting it was decided to launch a competition for the members, to write a series of essays, which would be published subsequently, on 'The Evil of

Unchastity' with a prize of one guinea for the best collection. Members were expected to subscribe a shilling a year and numerous meetings were held during this first year of the society.[24] Similarly, a society to reform morals was formed in Anglesey in 1853 and at an Eisteddfod in Porthmadog in 1851 the subject of the essay-writing competition was 'The most effective way of improving the morals and customs of the Welsh.''[25] No accounts survive of how successful these societies were in their aims and thus no assessments can be made of their true impact upon the courtship customs and practices of the youth of rural Wales. The impression one has is that they were imposed upon the young people from above by well-meaning but unsympathetic religious or social factions, and that their impact was probably localized and intermittent.

An eloquent correspondent to *Seren Gomer* in 1848 felt that a slightly different approach should be taken to the problem. He advocated the distribution of 2000 copies per area of an essay against 'Wales's greatest sin', in the form of a family booklet and costing under a penny, to complement the activities and aims of the parochial societies formed to stop courting in bed. The booklet would contain two pledges, the first of which should be signed by the head of the household himself, declaring:

> I promise that I will make every effort to find servants of good character in my house, and to prevent the custom of illegal bundling at night in the house in which I live. I also pledge that if I find a maid or maids guilty of bringing men into the house, for the above purpose, I shall turn them out of my service without pay at once. And also, I pledge that I will not receive into my service anyone who has previously lost his or her place because he/she was guilty of the custom named. I also promise, since marriage is honourable for all, and that it is necessary to socialize before marriage, that I will allow my servants adequate time for discourse with those they wish, for a reasonable period of time, and that before ten o'clock at night.

The second pledge was aimed at the household servants:

> I pledge that I will not follow the custom of lying illegally at night with anyone, and if I am found guilty of this, I promise I shall be willing to be turned out of my place of employment, without my wages.[26]

These articles in the denominational magazines reflected the opinions and attitudes of some of the most prominent clergy and preachers of the time. During the first half of the nineteenth century, Calvinistic Methodism was dominated by the famous preacher, John Elias of Anglesey, who strove valiantly, according to his biographer, to rid the country of 'such a loathsome custom'. For his efforts he was faced not only with opposition but with derision from those who ought to have supported him most stalwartly.[27] The editor of *Y Llan*, the Anglican Church's newspaper, on the other hand, reinforced the accusation made by William Roberts, the sexton of Llannor in an interlude in 1746, that the early Methodist societies promoted immorality and lust by presenting young people with 'a chance to play at covert-prostitution'.[28] Thus, in 1890 he stated that:

> Our Nonconformist brothers claim most of the inhabitants of Llŷn, Anglesey and Cardiganshire, and everyone knows that immorality is at its worst in these areas. What does one expect? We've heard of one elder who tried to attract a young girl to come to chapel instead of to Church as there were better facilities for finding a lover there![29]

These same arguments form the true theme of the novel *The Black Venus* by Rhys Davies, for although, superficially, it is the nonconformist heiress who courted in bed who is on trial for upholding the old practice, it is really a case of Church versus nonconformity in England and Wales.[30]

Those who advocated reform were, as in John Elias's case, often mocked and opposed. The Reverend T Miles Evans of Abergwili preached eloquently one Saturday night in 1891 against 'this evil' but met, not with understanding and sympathy but with derision. He was promptly chided for daring to raise his voice against the accepted customs of the area, especially as he was an outsider from another parish.[31]

Some religious congregations adopted the system of punishing individuals found guilty of engaging in this custom by expelling the young persons from the church or chapel. One Glamorganshire correspondent could boast with confidence, even as early as 1819, that any girl found courting the night in that area would lose her character forthwith; indeed, he claimed, no one had been expelled from his church for unchastity for over eighteen years.[32] Evidence, especially of a statistical nature, of such excommunications, is difficult to find and one must be content with impressions gained from fairly superficial knowledge. The Calvinistic Methodist, Reverend D Evans of Barmouth, discussed this matter before the *Commission on Labour, The Agricultural Labourer*, in 1893, and claimed that, in the annual reports of their monthly county meetings, continual references were made to unchastity as the chief cause of expelling members from the chapels. The percentages of persons excommunicated in Merionethshire in 1889 varied from 2.5 in Dyffryn, to 2.0 in Dolgellau, down to 1.6 in Ffestiniog.[33] Further information was gleaned in 1975 from a native of Abermeurig, Cardiganshire, who quoted the experiences of an old acquaintance who had himself been one of ten young people expelled from chapel for courting in bed during an evening meeting at the beginning of the century.[34] Likewise, the fate that would have faced Olwen in *The Black Venus*, would have been excommunication had courting in bed been declared a breach of conduct.

This novel would not have met with the approval of the nineteenth-century reformers as it tried to give a balanced view of the custom. In contrast, the novel *Mari Lewis, Y Wyryf Dwylliedig* (The Cheated Virgin) by the Reverend W Griffith, Pwllheli (1856) was written purely as propaganda. In this inelegant, uninspiring novel, typical of the early nineteenth-century *genre* in Wales, the custom of courting in bed is condemned totally, through the advice given to the misguided Mari Lewis by her wise fellow maid-servant Hannah Jones:

> Mari Lewis said that John Jones, son of Nant y Coed, was coming there on Friday night and she asked Hannah Jones whether she knew him,
>
> 'I believe that he is a young man who hasn't seen the evil of sin . . . and you should be on your guard with every such young man. Do you intend spending the whole night with him?'
>
> 'Why, Hannah Jones, don't you approve of that?'
>
> 'Not at all.'
>
> 'What would you like me to do?' asked Mary
>
> 'Well . . . spend an hour or two in the parlour with him before your parents go to bed.'
>
> 'Before my father and mother go to bed!Indeed, I wouldn't dream of doing that!'

'Why Mary?'

'I would be ashamed if they saw him'

'Ashamed if they saw him! . . . did you not own one another in view of the thousands at the fair yesterday? . . . I hope, dear Mary Lewis, if you decide to court the night that you don't intend lying down with him.'

'Why? it's not such an evil thing—that is the custom of this country.'

'Yes, yes, Mary Lewis . . . But remember that the fact that it is the custom of the country doesn't make it any less evil; and neither will the consideration that many others have engaged in this evil be of any help for the conscience to be upheld under the pressures of guilt in the world to come'.[35]

In a very similar vein the pros and cons of indulging in *caru ar y gwely* were finely balanced in a popular ballad of the period. In his *Ymddiddan rhwng Mab a Merch ynghylch myned i Garu ar y Gwely* (A Dialogue between a Lad and Lass about going Courting on the Bed) 'Bardus Lochwd' uses the boy to advocate retaining the custom and the girl to denounce it uncompromisingly. The young lad opens with a direct proposition:

Gad inni, Betti fach,
Gyd-orwedd yn y gwely,
Mae hon yn ffasiwn iach,
A difyr iawn i garu . . .

(Let us, dear Betty, Lie together in the bed, That is a healthy and very pleasant way to court.)

Why then, he asks, does Betty always listen to those who claim the custom to be harmful? In her reply, Betty admits that it is the custom of the country but that her parents oppose it completely. She does not wish to be left open to temptation. The boy then argues that it is as easy to be unchaste by the fire or in an outhouse as in bed, as in Nani Porth-y-rhos's case:

Trwy genad gyda'r nos
O'r diwedd gafodd faban.

(Through a call at night, At last she had a baby.)

To reinforce her argument the girl can call to mind several examples of ones who had fallen prey to the custom of courting in bed. Thus she suggests a different method:

Eisteddwch yma i lawr,
Yn wir mae ichwi groeso,
Mi 'rosaf bedair awr,
O flaen y tan i 'mgomio.

(Sit down here, Indeed you are welcome, I shall stay four hours To chat to you before the fire.)

The boy would not be deterred, however—for what of Beti Sion who had courted in bed for years and come to no harm? In spite of all his pleadings Betty remains calm and refuses to risk such a temptation:

Rhag ofn halogi'r tir
Na fu erioed mewn hadyd.

(Lest the land that has never been sown, be defiled.)

She concludes by reminding the lad that on the Day of Judgement he will be held responsible for his sins and for courting in bed.[36]

Betty's parents must have been among the new generation of guardians who wished to eliminate the old custom of courting the night. The traditional view was that the custom was fairly innocent and highly practical and that, as they themselves had indulged to the full in its charms when they were young, it would be hypocritical to wish to deprive their children, or other young people, of one of life's most pleasant experiences. Those who were heads of households also argued that it would be impossible to employ or keep servants in service unless they were allowed to go out courting when and where they wished. This was the comment made by the Reverend J W Trevor of Anglesey before the *Commission of Inquiry into the State of Education in Wales*, in 1847:

> They hire their servants agreeing to their stipulation for freedom of access for the purpose at stated times, or it may be, when they please.[37]

The vicar of Nefyn addressed the problem with grave determination:

> I have had the greatest difficulty in keeping my own servants from practising it. It became necessary to secure their chamber windows with bars to prevent them from admitting men. I am told by my parishioners that unless I allow the practice I shall very soon have no servants at all, and that it will be impossible to get any.[38]

The arguments of the reformers were obviously beginning to gather momentum and, as the century progressed, the issue of whether to court in bed or not began to form a wedge between the generations. The older generation began to wish it abolished, while the younger man- and maid-servants wanted to retain their independence in this matter. In his ballad praising the farm-servants of Wales the Bardd Crwst (1830-1901) condemned:

> . . . ambell i feistr a meistres
> Sy'n erbyn i'r forwyn yn wir,
> Gael dyfod â'i chariad i'r gwely,
> A hynny yn ffasiwn drwy'r sir.[39]

(. . . some masters and mistresses who are, indeed, opposed to the maid bringing her lover to the bed, Although that is the fashion throughout the county.)

On the other hand, the steadfast attempts of John Owen, Bethlehem, Anglesey, to prevent his servants from 'any irregular intercourse before marriage' were praised and admired in his obituary (1858) and his efforts seen as an example to others.[40]

Another Anglesey farmer decided to warn his maid-servants that they would be severely punished if they were caught in the act of courting in bed. The defiled bed would be carried out and burned in front of the whole household. Consequently, when a maid was found guilty, within a few days of this act, the following day, at midday, the bed and all the bed clothes were ceremoniously burned to a cinder. Significantly, the report notes that the maid was chided and mocked by her fellow workers during the 'ceremony'.[41]

Obviously some masters and fathers tried to keep a tight rein on their households. When one father was woken suddenly one night by a noise from his daughter's bedroom he got up at once to investigate. He grasped a large knife to challenge the intruder, but when he arrived at Mary's bedroom he found her a 'live picture of innocence' sitting on the bed meditating upon the Bible. The father, undeterred, sought out the lover, but in vain. Then he noticed that Mary was fidgeting with the bedclothes. He realized that the night visitor was lurking under the bed and having called him out, beat him fiercely, although he swore he wished to marry the girl. In his anger, the father would not listen or forgive and both the lover and the daughter were thrown out of the house forever.[42]

Such assaults could and did lead occasionally to court appearances and two examples of such cases, both associated with the village of Tre'r-ddôl, Cardiganshire, and within a few years of one another (between 1870 and 1875), illustrate how attitudes were gradually changing and hardening.

Two lads from Tre'r-ddôl set out one evening to court the night at Gwynfryn farm near Aberystwyth. Sometime during the night the farmer awoke and realized that there were *gwŷr caru* in the house. Evan Jenkins, one of the visitors, heard the father approach, so he got up, put on his coat and hat and tried desperately to escape through the door. The farmer caught him and beat him severely, although he protested vigorously that he had never courted in bed with any other girl and that they intended to be married that summer. After the event, the two youths decided to seek revenge for this demeaning experience and they brought a case of assault against the farmer. In court the farmer was found guilty of attacking the lovers without due cause and fined fifty pounds for each assault.[43]

Five years later a similar incident took place at Tre'r-ddol itself, but this time it was the farmer who accused a number of local youths of disturbing the peace of the neighbourhood by courting the night. For the time being the magistrates decided not to punish the lads with the proviso that they should remember that the justices and the police force would be determined to punish severely any found guilty of such an offence in future.[44]

This magisterial warning was not an idle one. When two lads were summoned before the court at Pwllheli in 1902 for disturbing the peace at Plas Bodegoes nearby, although the accused argued forcefully that they had merely been following the old tradition of going *i gynnig* (to attempt) and thence to court secretly in bed, the bench refused to listen to them and to deter them from repeating the practice they were fined and made to pay the costs of the case.[45] Indeed, the whole practice of 'going a-knocking' was coming under fire from the magistrates by this time. Daniel Rees, a farm servant of Llan-saint, was fined 3s 6d on 25 November 1905 for smashing a window at Tŷ'n-y-Bedw farm, for, having failed to attract his girlfriend's attention by throwing gravel, he began to throw cockles. Another farm-servant, Evan Jones of St Clears, in his frustration resorted to throwing half a brick at a window while courting in 1907 and was fined 3s 6d for his temerity.[46]

In view of all these attacks upon the old custom of courting the night, it is hardly surprising that it was gradually losing ground by the beginning of the twentieth century. The social and economic upheaval which came in the wake of the First World War dealt the last blow to the custom as it did to so many of the other traditions and rituals of rural Wales. It became perfectly acceptable now, for young couples to be seen out together by parents and masters and secretive, clandestine meetings were no longer necessary. The custom lingered on in the more remote areas for another decade and it has, therefore, been possible to locate one or two informants who claimed to speak with first-hand knowledge on the subject. The most eloquent of the speakers, Stephen Jones of Tŷ Mawr, Cilrhedyn, Pembrokeshire, could remember making appointments, *pwynts*, to court in bed with several of the young girls of his area. He would avoid Saturday night courting as this would interfere with his Sunday commitments. Although this informant revelled in his feats as a lover, his testimony shows that he understood the rules of the game and realized the significance of the tradition. In his opinion, it was between 1920 and 1930 that the Welsh custom of courting the night was finally routed from the traditional Welsh way of life.[47]

NOTES

[1]Stiles, p.109.
[2]W.F.M. Tape 4858, Mrs. J D Roberts, Brynllan, Llanllyfni.
[3]*Royal Commission on Labour,* p.32.

[4]*Y Dysgedydd,* 1834, p.211.
[5]*Baner ac Amserau Cymru,* 2/4/1880, p.14.
[6]*Reports of the Commissioners . . . Education in Wales,* Part I, 1847, pp.229,394.
[7]*Commission on the Employment of Children, Young Persons and Women in Agriculture,* (1867) Third Report of the Commissioners, (London, 1870), p.43.
[8]Russell Davies, 'In a Broken Dream, Some aspects of Sexual Behaviour and the Dilemmas of the Unmarried Mother in South West Wales, 1887-1914,' *Llafur,* vol.iii, 1983, p.25.
[9]Caradoc Evans, *My People*, p.135.
[10]Russell Davies, 'In a Broken Dream . . . ', p.26.
[11]G R Quaife, *Wanton Wenches and Wayward Wives,* p.98.
[12]Ibid, pp.218-9.
[13]*Baner ac Amserau Cymru,* 11/3/1891, p.5.
[14]Russell Davies, 'In a Broken Dream . . .', p.26.
[15]Russell Davies, 'Voices from the Void: Social Crisis, Social Problems and the Individual in South-West Wales, c.1876-1920', *Politics and Society in Wales, 1840-1922,* Essays in Honour of Ieuan Gwynedd Jones, ed. Geraint H Jenkins and J Beverley Smith, (Univ. of Wales Press, 1988), pp.81-91.
[16]Russell Davies, 'In a Broken Dream . . .', p.26.
[17]G R Quaife, *Wanton Wenches and Wayward Wives,* p.118.
[18]Russell Davies, 'In a Broken Dream . . .', p.32.
[19]Pembrokeshire Gaol Records, 1880-1881, Pembrokeshire County Record Office.
[20]*Seren Gomer,* 1818, p.136.
[21]*Yr Eurgrawn Wesleyaidd,* 1819, pp.372-6.
[22]*Seren Gomer,* 1840, p.379.
[23]*Y Dysgedydd,* pp.131-2; Scourfield, pp.103-5.
[24]*Yr Haul,* 1850, pp.290-2; 302, 370-1.
[25]W Gareth Evans, 'Y Ferch, Addysg a Moesoldeb. Portread y Llyfrau Gleision, 1847', P. Morgan (edit.) *Brad y Llyfrau Gleision* (Llandysul, 1991) p.97.
[26]*Seren Gomer,* 1848, p.45.
[27]Y Parch W Pritchard, *John Elias a'i Oes,* (Caernarfon, 1911), p.177.
[28]Geraint H Jenkins, *Hanes Cymru yn y Cyfnod Modern Cynnar, 1530-1760,* (Cardiff, 1983), p.307.
[29]*Y Llan a'r Dywysogaeth,* 25/4/1890, p.5.
[30]Rhys Davies, *The Black Venus*, (1944).
[31]*Baner ac Amserau Cymru,* 11/3/1891, p.5.
[32]*Yr Eurgrawn Wesleyaidd,* 1819, pp.372-6.
[33]*Royal Commission on Labour,* p.107.
[34]W.F.M. Mss 2120/2, D James Davies, Tai'n Cwm, Gartheli, Abermeurig.
[35]Emyr Wyn Jones, *Ysgubau'r Meddyg*, (Bala, 1973), pp.25-7.
[36]Bangor Mss xii, 89.
[37]*Reports of the Commissioners . . . Education,* 1847, p.536.
[38]Ibid., p.534.
[39]Bangor Mss, xxii, 151.
[40]*Y Drysorfa,* 1858, p.348.
[41]*Baner ac Amserau Cymru,* 19/2/1868, p.13.
[42]Ibid., 7/7/1869, p.11.
[43]Elfyn Scourfield, 'Fact Finding in a Welsh Rural Community', *Folk Life,* vol.x, (1972), p.65.
[44]*Baner ac Amserau Cymru,* 17/2/1875, p.10.
[45]Ibid., 17/12/1902, p.10.
[46]Russell Davies, p.25.
[47]Scourfield, 'Fact Finding . . .' pp.64-5.

Chapter 6

Courting Here and There

The art of courting, whether by night or by day, is, and always has been, very difficult and complex. Not surprisingly, therefore, all kinds of advice, all manner of charms and tests were devised to help the aspiring lovers to perfect their art. The most popular manual on the subject in the medieval period was *Ars Amatoria*, the work of the Latin poet, Ovid (43*BC*-*AD*18) who was court favourite until banished by Augustus. Although the Welsh medieval poets had probably never seen his work themselves, they were familiar, it seems, with its theme and contents. One anonymous fourteenth-century poet, in an effort to persuade a nun to disregard her chastity vows, advised her:

A chadw i'th gof lyfr Ofydd,
A phaid â gormod o ffydd.[1]

(And remember Ovid's book And don't indulge in too much faith.)

Likewise, Ieuan ap Rhydderch, a nobleman-poet from Cardiganshire, who had, possibly, attended Oxford University, claimed (in one of his fifteenth-century love poems) that he could remember Ovid's book well.[2]

In a much later period, young lovers, could, as today, turn to some of the popular magazines of the time to seek advice on courting techniques and discover, perhaps, in *Cyvaill yr Aelwyd* for 1888 an article by 'an experienced lover' on how to kiss:

> There is an art in kissing. It is not all nature's work . . . First of all decide whom you are going to kiss. Do not kiss at random, and never kiss for the sake of tradition. Don't leap for the fly like a trout. Take it slowly . . . Don't sit down to do the work . . .[3]

Although it is clear that this article was written with tongue in cheek, it does reflect the staidness of the Victorian image of courtship and can be contrasted sharply with the curious and perverse custom recorded during the same period from the Vale of Ceiriog whereby a man would try to prove his virility to his sweetheart to win her esteem. If the girl agreed to take part in the test, the lad would take her to a lonely, desolate place and ask her 'Do you wish to . . . *rhythu* (have a look)?' If she said 'yes', he would hold the brim of her hat between his teeth, then open the front part of his trousers and urinate on her dress. By exposing himself he was proving his virility to the young woman.[4]

Aspiring lovers could also try to stimulate the interest of the opposite sex by love charms and potions although, in many cases, they would have had to have been desperate to indulge in them. One unsavoury recipe associated with Carmarthensire was for the aspiring lover to cut off as much of his nails as possible and grind them into flour. They should then be mixed with something edible and given to the uncertain lad or lass to eat. There would be no further doubt who would be the object of his/her love.[5] Marie Trevelyan, on the other hand, discovered a pleasant concoction of metheglin, mead, rhubarb, cowslip, primrose or elderberry wine as her love potion but failed to abstract the mystery ingredient which ensured that the magic potion actually worked.[6] One would need the cooperation of one's heart's desire for the next charm to succeed, for the lad was urged to find two pieces of the devilsbit plant, one with five branches and one with three, and to place them for one day on his bosom. The following day he should endeavour to place them on her bosom and this charm would ensure her undying devotion.[7]

The course of true love rarely ran smoothly even with the knowledge of such charms and potions, for as the old Welsh saying maintains:

Wrth gicio a brathu
Mae cariad yn magu.[8]

(Love is nurtured by kicking and biting.)

A lover's sincerity and faithfulness could be tested in a number of ways. The worried partner could take a stem of fern and pluck the fronds one by one, counting each one in turn. If the number of fronds turned out to be an odd number, then their love was a steadfast and true one. The same charm was worked through the flower of the daisy. The interpretation of a similar charm using a peapod was a little different. In this case, two friends would work together and recite a set dialogue pattern. The lover would hold the pod and say a semi-nonsensical phrase, *Pysen lawn, abi dawn, abi delyn, abi danfon,* (Full peapod . . . send), his/her friend would then ask 'To whom?' was it to be sent and in reply the lover would name the chosen girl/lad. The next question would be 'How do you love her?' and the answer, before the pod would be opened, would be 'I love her a tiny, tiny amount, a very great deal:if he/she loves me as I love her/him, this peapod will contain an even number of peas'. The pod would be opened and if the number of peas proved to be even, the relationship was considered to be secure for the future.[9]

A similar love charm, using a set dialogue, was popular in the Middle Ages, as several love poems from the period illustrate. Iolo Morgannwg, the eighteenth-century Glamorganshire scholar and Romantic claimed that the custom of playing *cnau mewn llaw* (nuts in hand) was associated particularly with Halloween, but there is no further proof to support this.[10] According to the poets' descriptions the lover would send nuts to his/her beloved and the receiver would play *cnau i'm llaw* (nuts in my hand) with a partner. Thus, when Morfudd sent nuts to Dafydd ap Gwilym, the game proceeded thus: His partner held the nuts in the palm of his hand and said 'I have nuts in my hand', to which Dafydd replied, 'They are mine'. 'But why?' asked the partner, 'because they have been sent to me' was Dafydd's answer. 'From whom?' 'From . . .' (naming and describing Morfudd); 'Does she love you?' was the next question to which Dafydd answered, 'If she loves me there will be an odd number of nuts in your hand'. As might be expected, the number of nuts was an odd one, and Dafydd could then arrange an *oed mewn irgoed* (a date in luxuriant trees) with his beautiful Morfudd.[11] Iolo Goch, another fourteenth-century poet was not the receiver but the sender of nuts to his chosen one, but in this case they fell into the hands of her jealous husband, the *Eiddig*. When he realized that the number of nuts was nine, an odd number, the *Eiddig* became very angry and accused the poet and his wife of flaunting their love:

Fo a'th weled nos Wyl Fair,
Ti ac ef, mewn ty a gwair,
Ac a'th welad nos Ynyd,
Ti ac ef, mewn ty ac yd.[12]

(He had seen you on the eve of Mary's Feast day, You and he in a hay loft. And he had seen you on the eve of Shrove Tuesday, You and he in a corn barn.)

A poem by Ieuan ap Rhydderch has the same formula of question and answer as in Dafydd ap Gwilym's *cywydd*, and we see that in this case the girl is true to the poet as she has sent him seven nuts, an odd number, as a token of her affection.[13] It is interesting to note that in Devon a bride would be presented with a bag of nuts as she left the church after the wedding ceremony and that the phrase 'going-a-nutting' was considered to be an euphemism for love-making.[14]

Another method used for testing a lover's sincerity was to consult the magic properties of holy wells. Pins would be made from the thorns of the blackthorn and thrown into the water at Saeson well, Llanfihangel Bachellaeth, Caernarfonshire, and if they sank this proved that the lover was not sincere. At Cybi well, Llangybi, a kerchief would be spread on the water's surface and if it shifted to the right during the night the lover was known to be faithful and true in his love.[15]

Local girls on the Gower peninsula believed that the cromlech of Coetan Arthur on Cefn Bryn Common could help to work a similar charm. Until the end of the nineteenth century they used to meet at midnight around this stone when the moon was full. On the stone a cake of barley-meal and honey, mixed with milk would be placed. To test the fidelity of their lovers the girls would crawl three times around the stone on their hands and knees and if their lovers were faithful, it was believed that they would soon join them.[16]

The most popular test of a lover's intentions was associated with the birch tree. Indeed the birch was extremely significant in the folklore of courtship throughout the centuries. The love poems of the medieval poets contain many references to seeking to court girls under the green leaves of the birch tree. They seek an *oed dydd* (a date by day) (in direct contrast, perhaps, in summer, to the custom of courting the night in winter) with the girls and try to draw them out into the *bedwlwyn* (birchgrove). Llywelyn ap y Moel wrote a poem to the *bedwlwyn* itself urging it to bear forth leaves after the winter months so that he could meet his beloved under its branches once more.[17] An anonymous fifteenth-century poet describes the 'house' he had formed for his secret rendezvous:

A house I made to love her
Under the birch, no fool's venture.
I trimmed a noble clearing,
Plaited praise, built in a ring,
Where leaf and lithe twigs covered,
Like tiles the thick bowl of wood.

Two thrushes, love birds, came to tenant this leafy house and, as so often in medieval love poems, the poet diverts his attention to describing them and the beauty of nature. He returns to his original theme towards the end of the poem and vows:

I want for a splendid sweetheart
In this dwelling place to hold court,
Unless I have a fair maid,
My own age, in the birch glade,
Nevermore (I put this ban)
I'll build for love of woman.[18]

As with the courting at night, the aim of the 'daytime date' was to form a comfortable bed for the lovers to court on the birch leaves and twigs. Certainly this was Dafydd ab Edmwnd's intention when he built

'gaer oed dydd gorau tyddyn
gwyrdd a dail i guddio dyn . . .
awn i gael yn y gwely
araith gan y fronfraith fry
cydgysgu cydbrynu braint
cydorwedd lle ceid erwaint . . .'[19]

(a fortress for daytime dating, the best dwelling, greenery and leaves to hide one . . . let us go to hear, in bed, a song from the thrush above; to sleep together, to buy freedom together, to lie together where the meadowsweet grows . . .)

Lovers in the countryside—courting in the birch groves.
(Bibliothèque Nationale)

Courting in the woodland.

(Bibliothèque Nationale)

Yet again, Bedo Brwynllys, another fifteenth-century poet, states clearly that his house of birch (and hazel in this case) was built with one purpose only in mind:

> *Mynnwn, a hwn yw fy nhŷ*
> *Gael hon i'r gwely hynny.*[20]

(I shall insist on getting her into that bed, and this is my house.)

The freedom associated with courting in the countryside contrasted vividly with the difficulties and restrictions imposed on the lovers by the conventions of 'going a knocking'. It was also in complete contrast with the disciplined rituals associated with 'courtly love' which were so popular with the upper-classes and which looked upon women as perfect but untouchable ideals. These 'birch' poems echo the French pastourelles, poems which describe the poet roaming the countryside, meeting by chance a rustic girl and trying to seduce her. In most cases the girl resists but is eventually overcome by force. However, in line with medieval church thinking, girls were believed to have a more sensual nature than men, the final outcome could be that the girl would be secretly grateful to the man for seducing (not raping) her. The poem 'Sexual Intercourse' belongs to this genre and reflects these attitudes. The poet has failed, in this instance, to woo the girl courteously but when he meets her in the woods he takes her by force:

> Until noon I grappled at close quarters
> with the beauty under the trees
> and pushed my friendly girl
> down under the green birch
> and shoved her onto her back,
> my moon, with her legs apart . . .
> and drove my pleasure
> until its tip reached the end of her box . . .[21]

These same, medieval poets also note that objects made from birch twigs and leaves served as symbols of love when exchanged between lovers. The most popular token of affection in the period was the *cae bedw* (the birchen garland):

Coedyn bach o rwym ceudawd
Crefft hysbys rhwng bys a bawd.[22]

(A small twig of hollow binding, skilfully crafted between finger and thumb.)

Dafydd ap Gwilym, in another poem, sings praise to Madog's *cae bedw*. The Madog in question was Madog Benfras, a contemporary Welsh poet, who, it seems, had received a birchen garland from his beloved. He wore the garland *am ei ben . . . beunydd* (on his head . . . every day). Another poet, Iorwerth ab y Cyriog, however, had received a ring of gold from his sweetheart but Dafydd criticized him for courting the girl for her money rather than for her love as Madog had done.[23] It is worth noting, although the statement cannot be authenticated, that Iolo Morgannwg claims that Madog Benfras had won a chair and a *cae bedw* in an Eisteddfod in the time of Edward III for a love poem.[24] On another occasion, Dafydd ap Gwilym asked his girlfriend of *unoed* (one date) to prove her love for him by making him a garland of leaves. She, however, refused, for it would be cruel to denude the birch tree of its leaves and she would prefer to present him with a garland of peacock feathers instead.[25] Dafydd ab Edmwnd also received a *cae bedw* as a token of love from both Gwen Hwlyn of Hanmer parish and Cari Mwyn and wrote, in each case, a poem to thank them for the tokens of their affection. He emphasized too, that the girls made the garlands themselves, by *cyd-bwyso coed a'u bysedd,* (balancing wood with their fingers).[26]

Dafydd ap Gwilym has a poem to say thank you for a *het fedw* (a birchen hat) and although it is not clear what the exact difference is between a *cae fedw,* a garland of birch twigs worn around the head, and the birchen hat, Dafydd indicates, that they were tokens of varying affection. The birch hat was worn when the lover had been faithful to his girlfriend for *cannoed* (a hundred dates).[27]

The custom of making elaborate garlands or hats from birch twigs seems to have declined gradually and a simpler custom taken its place; for it was common by the nineteenth century for the aspiring lover to send merely a branch or twig of the birch tree to his beloved as a token of his affection. The youths of Glyntraean parish in the Vale of Ceiriog, for example, used to carry birch twigs stripped of their bark as they travelled the area on their night-courting missions.[28] All these examples emphasize the significance of the birch tree in courtship folklore. It is apposite to remember, too, that the Maypole in Wales was often called *bedwen haf* (summer birch) and that dancing around the *bedwen haf* on May Day and at Midsummer was both a fertility rite and a celebration of youthful love.

T Llew Jones has added another dimension to this discussion through his recent research on birch besoms. It appears that if a young lass, a spinster or a widow, were to place a besom in an obvious place outside her front door, the local men and lads would know at once that it had been placed there as a sign that they would be welcome to call at the house as lovers. He quotes the traditional rhyme:

Propor gorff, ai ti sy yna?
Dod dy draed ar lawr yn ara',
Gwylia daro wrth yr ysgub,
Ysgafn iawn yw cwsg fy modryb.

(Chaste body, is it you? Place your feet down slowly, Lest you should strike against the besom, My aunt sleeps very lightly.)

Certainly the besom was used in this manner in Huntingdonshire, England, where 'Everbody knowed . . . it were a recognised signal', while in Somerset if a wife were to leave her husband, his friends would tie a besom to his chimney as a sign that he could do with a new woman.[29]

This custom in turn reminds one of 'besom weddings' whereby a birchen besom would be placed across an open doorway with the head of the broom on the threshold. The youth would then jump over the besom and the girl would follow immediately. In this way they would have performed a ritual which was accepted as a common law wedding rite. This kind of wedding was common not only amongst gypsies but also throughout rural Wales well into the nineteenth century.[30] In some areas it was believed that if a girl inadvertently walked over a besom of birch twigs she would conceive out of wedlock. Naturally, therefore, village youths would play practical pranks on local girls by laying down besoms across their paths.[31]

If the young lad were to give or send a birchen twig or branch to his chosen one he could hope, if she cared for him, to receive a birchen twig in return. If, however, the girl wished to end the relationship and show her decision symbolically, she would send a different type of twig back to him. The hazel was the species usually chosen for this unpleasant task. The hazel branch, stripped of its bark, would be a *ffonwen* (a white stick) and, in order to emphasize its message, it was often decorated with black mourning ribbon and accompanied by a satirical verse. The verse would be a piece 'of homespun poetry, setting forth the significance of the article transmitted, with also sundry complimentary references to the person addressed, as "being on the shelf", and other pointed pin-pricks calculated to open old sores and to wound the too susceptible feeling of a "good-old-has-been"'.[32] It was not always the girl who sent this sign of refusal; it was often the lover's friends who chose to mock the loser by sending the *ffonwen* to him on the day of his former girlfriend's marriage to her new partner. Thus, when Dafydd ap Gwilym was jilted by Morfudd, he found himself to be the butt of his friends' ridicule for they gave him 'twigs of fresh hazel'.[33] Likewise, Sion Tudur, a sixteenth-century poet, hated the hazel twigs he had so rudely received from his girlfriend in return for his token of love—the birch twig, and warned others of the dangers:

Oer oedd cael, heb arwydd ced,
Irwydd cyll, arwydd colled . . .
Na roed yr ifanc na'r hen
Galar fyd, goel ar fedwen;
Canmawl bedwen heb weniaith
Collen fydd dyben y daith.[34]

(It was cruel to receive, without sign of a gift, a fresh twig of hazel, a symbol of loss . . . Let neither young nor old, sorrowful world, place their trust in the birch; If one praises the birch without flattery, the end of the journey will be a hazel twig.)

In like manner, Salbri Powell, in the same period, suffered greatly as 'an ailing poet', when his love went 'flibbertigibbet' at the hands of mocking friends:

And now, no lad's so simple
Or lusty cheery damsel
But's glad enough to joke and pick
And hand me a stick of hazel.

Undaunted, however, he decided to put the sticks of hazel to good use and to try to win his only love back again in the fullness of time:

In Gwaun y Plu I'll gather
And plant each stick together;
If you can trust an old wives' tale
The twigs can't fail to prosper.

Thus he would form a 'new dwelling' of the twigs and branches of the hazel:

And when the nuts shall ripen
And the birds sing their burden
Fairer than fair she'll come therein
Like a linnet in my garden . . .

And there I'll be desiring
A bed, in shelter hiding,
To have, O lovely form, with her
A skilful, tender loving.[35]

Such determined optimism was the key to Alun Mabon's success as wooer of Menna Rhen in J Ceiriog Hughes's famous nineteenth-century pastoral poem. Alun Mabon sent Menna a birchen branch but she returned a hazel branch to him. However:

Ond chaiff y gangen fedwen
Ddim gwywo'n goch ei lliw
Nes af i siarad eto
Yng ngwyneb Menna wiw.[36]

(But the birchen branch will not be allowed to wither red in colour
Until I go again to speak face to face with fair Menna.)

Does this perhaps suggest that if the unsuccessful lover were to bid for the girl again, before the twig of birch withered, he could hope to be successful at his second attempt?[37]

The use of the *ffonwen* custom, although often merely horseplay, could be cruel to the jilted lover. In the Llansilin and Dyffryn Banw areas of Powys, it would be sent by post to arrive on the morning of the wedding and as it was so easy to guess the contents of such a package, the poor victim would be derided mercilessly.[38] A north Pembrokeshire verse on the subject advised the victim not to be too downhearted but to remember the 'other fish in the sea'.

Mae Twm Penfigyn wedi colli'i gariad,
Mae cur yn ei galon a dŵr ar 'i lygad;
Rhowch help iddo gered a halwch iddo ffonwen,
Ceith nosweth o garu gida Shan Pantyronnen.[39]

(Twm Penfigyn has lost his sweetheart; he has a heartache and tears in his eyes; Offer him help to walk and send him a white stick. He can have a night courting with Shan Pantyronnen.)

The hazel was not the only wood used in this way, as a token of rejected love. Indeed, as it was customary to make a garland or hat of birch to mark affection so it was common to symbolize refusal and rejection by presenting the jilted lover with a *cap/het helyg* (a willow cap or hat).[40] This cruel custom is described by an eighteenth-century diarist, William Thomas of Llanfihangel-ar-Elai, Glamorganshire, for as he comments that the parish church bells were chimed one day to celebrate the birth of a son to one of the parish girls he adds, 'a willow was made for Thomas Rich her late wooer'.[41]

The well-known Welsh folk-song *Y Ferch o Blwy Penderyn* (The Lass from Penderyn Parish) refers to this custom. The song describes the lover being informed by a bird on his way to work that his girlfriend has found another man. In his consternation the lover faints:

Ond pwy ddaeth yno, er fy nghwyno,
Onid pryfyn oddiar y pren
A chap o helyg ffein digynnyg
I mi gael mwrnio ar ol Gwen.[42]

(But who came there, in spite of my ailing, But a bird from on the tree With a fine unsolicited willow cap So that I could mourn after Gwen.)

The willow, of course, and the weeping willow in particular, was often used as a symbol of death, and, in this case, of the death of love. The custom seems to have barely survived into this century as D J Williams' comments upon the courting adventures of his Uncle Jâms in rural Carmarthenshire illustrate:

> I have a vague memory too of the fun in the house when one of the maids placed a willow cap on his head the morning Elen y Wenallt, one of his old sweethearts, got married . . . I heard the custom mentioned several times afterwards, but that was the only time I knew one to be presented, in accordance with an age-old ritual, to the disappointed wooer.[43]

There were several other objects that symbolized rejection in love. In west Carmarthenshire the jilted lover might receive yellow flowers and if there were no yellow flowers available he would be sent a yellow ribbon or cloth as a signal.[44] One informant from the same area who served as a pig-slaughterer in Cwm-bach, Whitland during the winter months remembered the custom of sending 'a pig's tail through the post' to a jilted lover.[45] There are examples of sending onions too[46] and numerous references to the symbolic meaning of receiving ginger. In Nantlle Vale, Caernarfonshire, roots of ginger would be tied together here and there along a piece of string and sent, unwrapped and anonymously, of course, with only the address on a piece of card.[47] One informant from Cemaes, Anglesey, could testify that he saw a bachelor farm-servant at the farm where he was a young servant receive a package by post one day containing a piece of ginger, an onion, a black tie and a pair of girl's stockings to remind him that his previous girlfriend was getting married that day to another suitor.[48]

Similar practices were popular in other parts of Britain. In Cold Aston, Derbyshire, a former sweetheart found the wedding garland, decorated with a bottle of urine and an onion, hung outside his house the morning of the wedding, while abandoned lovers in Cumberland would have been 'comforted' by being seized and rubbed with 'pease straw'.[49]

The terms for rejection and being rejected vary in Welsh. If he were the victorious lover he was said to have *rhedag hwn a hwn* (run so and so); while if he were the abandoned lover he 'would have been run' *wedi cael ei redag*[50]; *wedi cael cwd*[51]; or *wedi cael cawell*[52]; (literally to have had a purse/basket). This last saying is found in traditional Welsh verses:

Cawell neithiwr, cawell echnos,
Cawell heno'n hur ddiachos.
Os caf gawell nos yfory
Rhoddaf ffarwel byth i garu.

(Rejection last night, rejection the night before, Rejection tonight without good cause. If I am rejected tomorrow night I shall give up courting forever.)

Nid af i garu'r nos ond hynny,
Cefais gawell ym Mynachdy;
Rwyf yn canmol synnwyr Sioned
Am ei roddi gyn gynhared.[53]

(I shall not go courting the night again, I was rejected at Mynachdy; I have to praise Sioned's common sense for being so prompt in her rejection.)

The rejected lover would not always submit to this ridicule without seeking revenge. In the Llanfair Pwllgwyngyll area of Anglesey, a forsaken wooer would make an effigy of his successful rival on May Eve and would then place it in a prominent position, *crogi gŵr gwellt* (to hang a straw effigy) near the unfaithful girl's home. A letter would be pinned to the effigy and the quarrel between the two men would often be resolved in a fight at the Llannerch-y-medd May fair.[54] In true Cardiganshire style, a rejected lover from that county decided on a far more practical method to express his jealousy and claim compensation for the anguish he had suffered. He sent a bill of all his expenses on his former girlfriend to her new sweetheart and this was published in the Welsh newspaper *Baner ac Amserau Cymru* in 1869. As the bill contains items which illustrate vividly some of the customs described in previous chapters, it is worth quoting in full:

	£	s	d
For 53 glasses of wine in different fairs and markets at 3d each		13	3
For one pair of leather gloves		4	6
For one pair of shoes, and heeling two old ones that I wore out as I walked back and fore to . . .		19	6
To Jac the blacksmith for nails for the above		3	4
To Dr . . . for curing the cough I caught from waiting under the window for you on a wet night to come from your bed to open to me	9	9	9
For postage		1	11
For deceiving me and throwing me out of 'life's companionship'	100	0	0
For 'drawing' me . . . 99 times, at 2s 6d a time	12	7	6
For losing 12 days in your company	4	14	0
	£128	14	9[55]

If the bill, at this second time of asking, was not paid immediately, the sender threatened to sue the debtor forthwith!

There is little evidence that rejected girlfriends were the objects of such ridicule and derision by their friends and peers. Yet in their lovesick condition they often turned to the most unpleasant remedies to seek a cure for a broken heart. In Caernarfonshire, the girl would catch a live frog and stick pins into it before throwing it into a lake to die. When the frog had died the girl would be cured of her sickness.[56] On Cardiganshire's Mynydd Bach, *c.*1829, a woman said to be suffering from love trouble was cured in the most bizarre way by an old maid of the area. A piece of lead was put in a ladle to melt. The patient was laid on her back on the floor and a tub placed on her chest. Water was poured into this tub and the molten lead into the water. The woman, cured of her sickness, got up and lived to be seventy.[57] According to tradition, Nansi Clandwr, from the same county, could claim a very effective remedy for lovesickness. It involved the repetition of certain words and was followed by a drink concocted of gin, beer and saffron.[58] Indeed, making love charms and curing lovesickness were standard items in the repertoire of almost every local wise woman and they were consulted with great faith.

Many of the rites and customs described in this chapter seem unnecessarily cruel to us today, yet they should and must be seen within their true social context. Rites of rejection symbolized the original breach in relationship between two former lovers and thus deterred further attempts after marriage to try to *ail-gynnau tân ar hen aelwyd* (re-kindle fire on an old hearth).

NOTES

[1]C T B Davies, 'Cerddi'r Tai Crefydd', Unpublished University of Wales MA Thesis, 1972, vol.i, no.5.
[2]Henry Lewis, Thomas Roberts, Ifor Williams, *Cywyddau Iolo Goch ac Eraill,* (Cardiff, 1972), Lxxvi.
[3]*Cyvaill yr Aelwyd,* 1888, p.134.
[4]W Rhys Jones, W.F.M. Mss 2593,pp.84-5.
[5]Williams, p.352.
[6]Trevelyan, p.238.
[7]*Cymru,* 1903, vol.xxv, p.143.
[8]Oral testimony Eifion Glyn Roberts, Pen-y-groes, Caernarfon.
[9]Williams, p.355.
[10]G J Williams, *Iolo Morgannwg,* (1956), p.39.
[11]*GDG,* 50, pp.485-6,557.
[12]Lewis, Roberts, Williams, xxi.
[13]Ibid., Lxxvi.
[14]J H Wilks, *Trees of the British Isles in History and Legend,* (London, 1972), pp.125-6.
[15]T Gwynn Jones, p.114; *Llafar Gwlad,* no.17, p.10.
[16]Robin Gwyndaf, *Chwedlau Gwerin Cymru/Welsh Folk Tales* (Cardiff, 1989), p.87.
[17]Lewis, Roberts, Williams, Lxii.
[18]*Welsh Verse,* pp.190-1.
[19]Thomas Roberts, (edit.) *Gwaith Dafydd ab Edmwnd,* p.5.
[20]Donovan, p.22.
[21]D. Johnston, . . . *Medieval Welsh Erotic Poetry*, p.55.
[22]*GDG,* 38.
[23]Ibid., 31.
[24]*Y Bywgraffiadur Cymreig hyd 1940,* (London, 1953), p.572.
[25]*GDG,* 32.
[26]Thomas Roberts, pp.10-11, 12-3.
[27]*GDG,* 59, p.492.
[28]W Rhys Jones, W.F.M. Mss 2593, p.71.
[29]*Llafar Gwlad,* No.4 1984.
[30]W Rhys Jones, 'Besom Wedding in the Ceiriog Valley', *Folk-Lore,* 34, (1928), pp.149-60.
[31]Wilks, p.124.
[32]*Bye-gones,* 21 Dec., 1898.
[33]*GDG,* 85.
[34]*Y Brython,* 1860, p.65.

[35]*O.B.W.V.*, 110; *Welsh Verse*, p.146.
[36]T Gwynn Jones, *Ceiriog*, (Wrecsam, 1927), p.146.
[37]Letter from Mrs. Anne Evans, Rhydau Gloewon, Llithfaen, Pwllheli, 'Ar Gof a Chadw', Radio Cymru, 28/1/85.
[38]*W.F.C.*, pp.158-9; Letter from Ted Williams, 2 Trem Menai, Bangor, 'Ar Gof a Chadw', Radio Cymru, 13/2/85.
[39]Morris, p.133.
[40]*GDG*, 85.
[41]Cardiff Mss4.877, p.165.
[42]W.F.M. Mss 1737/13.
[43]D J Williams, p.111.
[44]Williams, p.356.
[45]Oral testimony, Tom Morgans, Sarnau, Cwm-bach, Carmarthenshire.
[46]*Llafar Gwlad*, no.17, p.21.
[47]Ibid., no.18, p.5.
[48]Oral testimony, Bob Lewis, Carreg Lefn, Cemaes, 'Ar Gof a Chadw', Radio Cymru, 1985.
[49]Gillis, p.73.
[50]B Lewis Jones and D Llwyd Morgan,(edit.), *Bro'r Eisteddfod 3, Ynys Mon*, p.36. W H Jones, p.74.
[51]W.F.M. Mss 3472/2, Mary Jones, Pennant.
[52]B Lewis Jones, *Iaith Sir Fôn*, (1984), p.20.
[53]*HB*, 464, 463.
[54]*W.F.C.*, pp.98-9.
[55]*Baner ac Amserau Cymru*, 26/5/1869, p.14.
[56]John Jones, (Myrddin Fardd), p.259.
[57]*Y Geninen*, vol.xiv, p.194.
[58]Gillis, p.73.

Chapter 7

Love Tokens

Giving, or exchanging, love tokens was one of the main conventions of the traditional art of courtship. We have already noted that attractive maidens would be inundated with gifts or fairings at local fairs and how the birchen twig and the willow hat symbolised the expression of love, but there were many other gifts associated with love and courting. We have little evidence how these gifts would be presented, though it would be fair to surmise that the *gwas caru*, or courtship attendant, played a prominent role at this stage of a courtship. References have been found also to *ceiswyr*, (seekers) who would lead young women by the hand to a secluded corner to deliver the gift on behalf of an ardent admirer. [1]

It is also difficult to ascertain the exact significance of each gift. Were they merely tokens of affection or did they symbolize a more lasting relationship, as the engagement ring purports to do today? Henry Best, a Yorkshire yeoman of the 1640s, in his detailed account of courtship customs, suggests that each visit was accompanied by a love token but that they would be presented at random:

> He perhaps giveth her a ten-shilling piece of gold, or a ring of that price or perhaps a twenty-shilling piece, or a ring of that price, then the next time, or the next time after that, each other time, some conceited toy or novelty of less value. [2]

Thus it was not the value of the gift but the giving and acceptance that mattered. Macfarlane maintains that marriage litigation confirms how important the practice of giving love tokens in sealing a bond between two lovers was and quotes examples from the sixteenth and seventeenth centuries in England. [3] But in Wales it proves difficult to pinpoint certain objects and claim that they had lasting significance, especially since, up until the nineteenth century, the boundary between courtship and marriage, between the betrothal and the actual nuptuals was extremely fine and difficult to define.

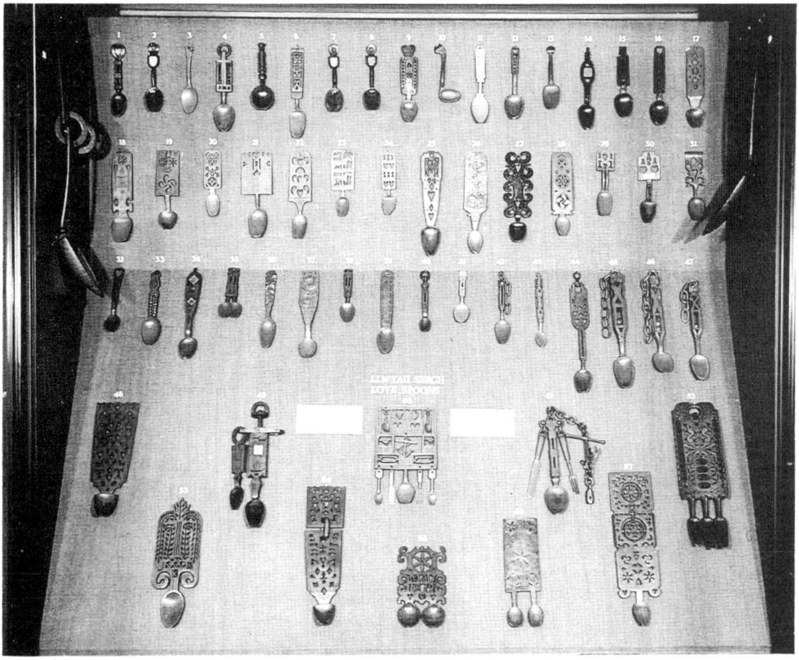

Love spoons
Notice the intricate carvings of symbols of love & fruit, birds and leaves; the chain links, the wooden caging and the slotted balls.
(Welsh Folk Museum)

The love token that has attracted most attention in Wales is the traditional love-spoon. Much has been written and romanticized about the custom of giving a love-spoon to one's sweetheart, yet its origins and a satisfactory analysis of its development continue to elude the historian. Spoons have been decorated and given as presents for centuries and in many countries though there is no definite theory why they became popular.[4] The term 'spooning' means:

> to be close together, to fit into each other, in the manner of spoons; to make love, especially in a sentimental or silly fashion.[5]

It is uncertain whether it is actually derived from the custom although such an explanation would seem plausible. On the other hand, the south-west Wales dialect term for boyfriend,

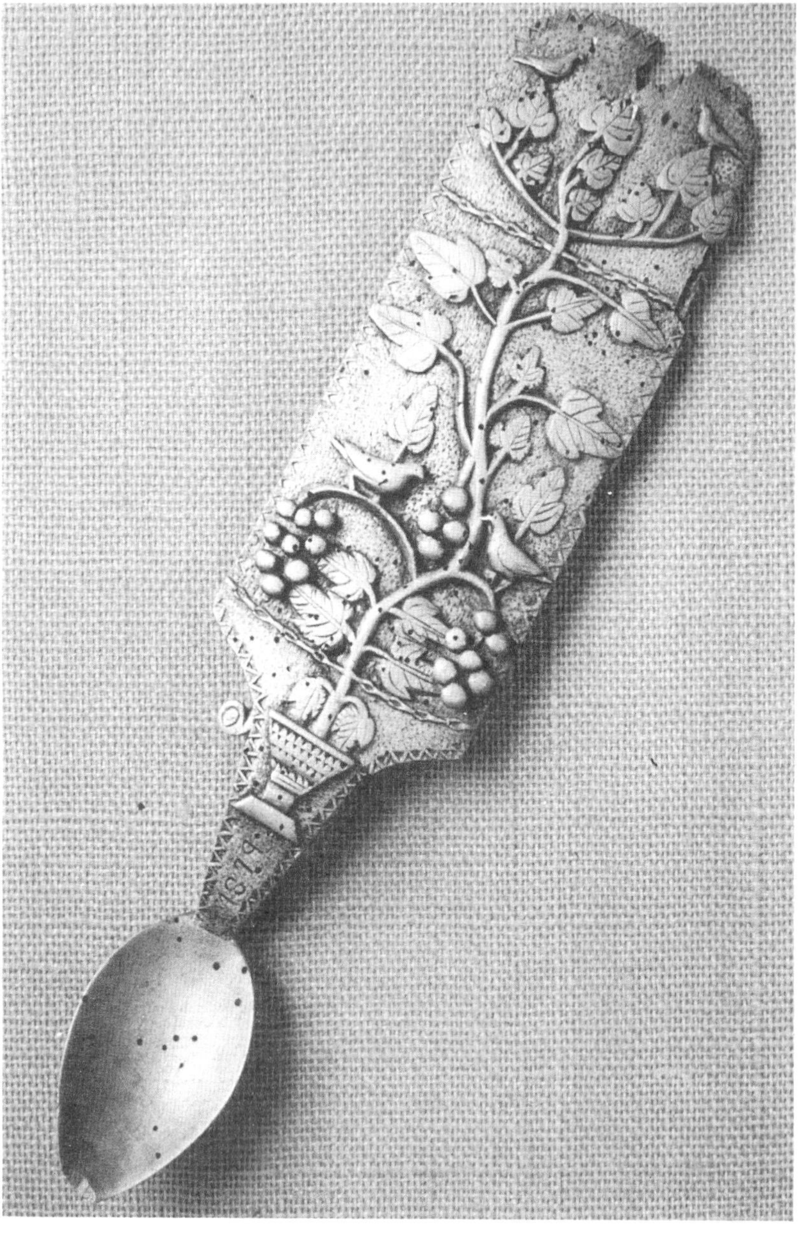

Detail of carving on a love-spoon.
(Welsh Folk Museum)

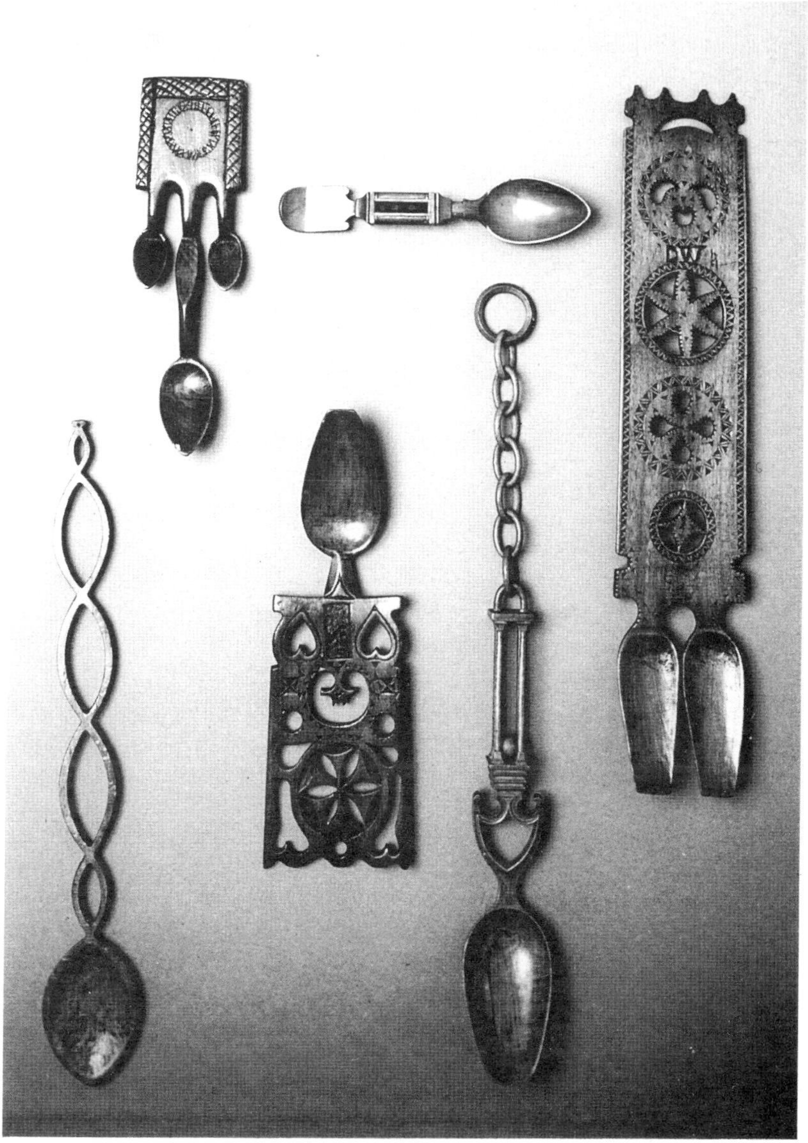

Love-spoons.

(Welsh Folk Museum)

sboner, can surely be associated with love-spoons. It is more difficult to explain how a girlfriend came to be called a *wedjen* 'a wedge' in the same dialect,though there may be some link with 'wench' a common name for a young damsel or maid-servant.

The first examples of love-spoons in museums and private collections date from the seventeenth century.[6] There is no documented evidence to prove that the custom was popular before this period. There can be no doubt, however, that the custom became increasingly popular from the seventeenth century to the nineteenth century. The craft of making domestic spoons had been carried on in Wales at least since the medieval period and the first love-spoons were merely more intricate versions of the utilitarian versions found in the home. Although many examples are undated, and indeed undatable, some craftsmen did choose to carve the date on their spoons. The earliest dated specimen in the Welsh Folk Museum's collection was made in 1667. It has a square slotted stem-handle which has been hollowed out leaving small wooden balls running freely in the cavity. It is of a fairly elaborate design suggesting that it was certainly not the first love-spoon to be made. The earliest spoons would probably have been used for eating but gradually, as they became more and more decorative and larger in size they became unwieldy and impractical for daily use.

Most of the love-spoons were carved by the lovers themselves and the use of initials emphasizes their intimate and personal message. They sought, through their craftsmanship, to express their romantic feelings of love and caring, for, the more intricate and decorative the spoon, the deeper the love it purported to symbolize. The simple functional love-spoon could be elaborated in several ways. The handle could be enlarged into a rectangular-shaped panel which allowed detailed carvings. Geometrical designs were generally favoured as they were easier to carve but other motifs, such as circles, keyholes, birds, vines and locks were also popular. Sailors who spent long hours on voyages across the seas often decorated their love-spoons with anchors and ships. Occasionally, the motifs were topical such as the carving of Telford's Menai Suspension Bridge on a spoon dated 1825. The craftsman could use fretwork and poker-work to vary the design and occasionally spoons displayed a red or black wax inlay.

Another method of decorating the handle would be to form a slotted cage of wood with loose balls running freely inside it. It has been suggested, though not conclusively, that the number of balls symbolized the number of children the carver hoped for after marriage. Chain links would often be attached to these elaborate handles, another indication that the love-spoon had developed into a purely ornamental object. One example found today in a private collection at Aberaeron, Dyfed, was made in 1840 by one William Williams of Maentwrog, to celebrate his forthcoming betrothal to Frances Llwyd. The spoon was made of holly wood and has a knife, spoon and fork hanging from a central yoke which is attached to a beautiful chain containing 135 links.[7] The fact that the links and balls were carved out of a single block of wood and not made up of individual pieces reveals the ingenuity and skill of the carver.

To balance the enlarged handle the craftsman would choose to replace the single bowl with a double or even a triple bowl. Double bowls were common in the Llanwrtyd area of Breconshire and symbolized *Yr ydym ni ein dau yn un* (We two are one).[8] In spite of this example, however, it is usually difficult to identify regional types. The original collectors forgot to record their provenance and it is impossible now to locate most of them or to prove that certain fashions belonged to certain areas. Yet it can be loosely maintained that plain spoons with small glazed recesses in the handles were found particularly in Caernarfonshire and that those of Pembrokeshire tended to have double panels linked rather clumsily by a loop.

During the nineteenth century and well into the twentieth it became customary to set competitions in *Eisteddfodau* on making wooden spoons and occasionally love-spoons. A prize of ten shillings was offered for the 'Best Collection of Wooden Spoons made with a knife by farm labourers' in the Cardiff Royal Eisteddfod in 1899,[9] and one D Lewis, Ffostrasol, Ceredigion, won first prize for a love-spoon at the 1937 Llangeitho Eisteddfod.[10] This indicates that such objects were becoming rarer and falling more and more into the sphere of the specialized wood carver, who took to carving as a challenging hobby, rather than to the farm-labourer who wished to express his most intimate emotions through the medium of the love-spoon. This is the case today as love-spoon galleries and shops sprout into being throughout Wales to display the work of craftsmen, who carve their love-spoons for money and decoration, rather than as personal symbols of love.

Several other carved wooden objects would serve as love tokens during this period. Knitting was a favourite domestic craft amongst young women, and yarn hooks and knitting sheaths would have been acceptable gifts, not only for their expression of love, but for practical purposes. Yarn hooks were shaped as an elaborate S, one hook being suspended from the apron waist-band and the other holding the ball of wool. This would enable the knitter to walk while knitting. In the Welsh Folk Musuem collection there is a wide variety of brass, copper and other metal yarn hooks. Some of the wooden examples are intricately carved with initials and dates and heart-shaped

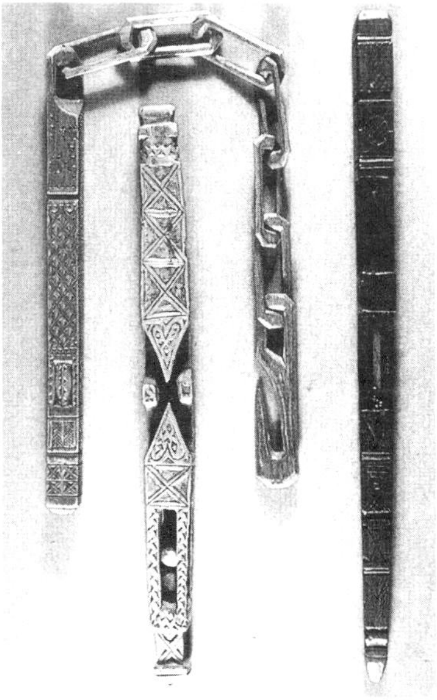

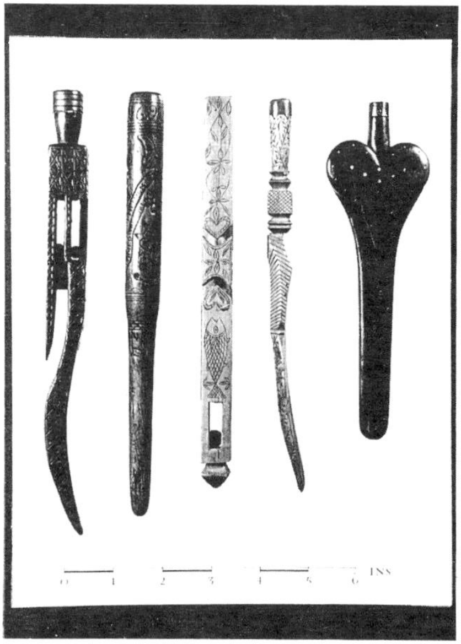

Knitting sheaths
They would be thrust into the waistband on the right hip to hold one knitting needle, thus freeing one hand to continue with other housework.
Again notice the intricate carvings.
(Welsh Folk Museum)

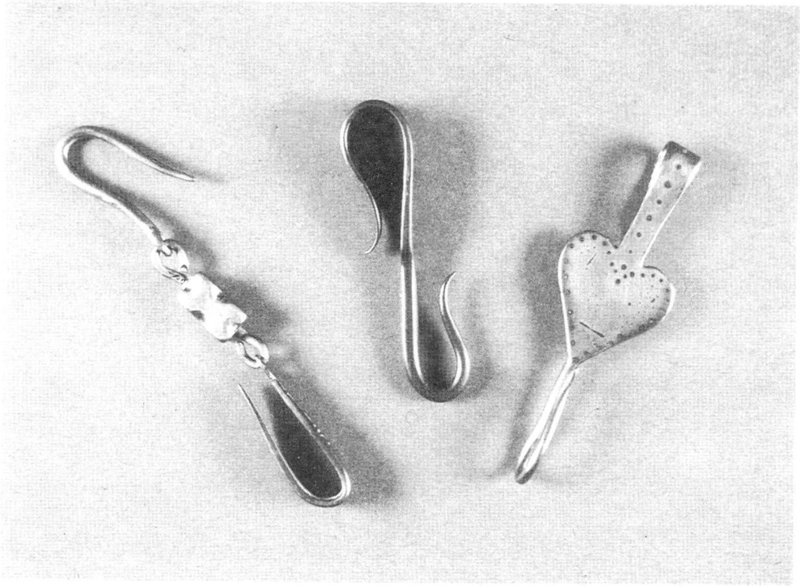

Waist yarn hooks
They were suspended from the waistband to hold the ball of wool.
(Welsh Folk Museum)

decorations to prove that they were originally presented as love tokens. Knitting sheaths or sticks were usually worn, tucked into the strings of the apron, on the right hip. The right needle would be placed in the bore and the right hand placed close up over the needle point allowing the forefinger to act as a shuttle.[11] Knitting was associated originally with the working classes, but gradually during Victorian times it became accepted into the Victorian parlour and ivory, metal and brass knitting sheaths became common. The earliest dated Welsh specimen in the collection was made in 1680 and it is certain that the most elaborately carved were intended as tokens of affection and love.

Stay busks, 'a strong piece of wood, or whalebone, thrust down the middle of the Stomacher to keep it streight and in compass that the Breast nor Belly shall not swell too much out',[12] were commonly worn during the seventeenth and eighteenth centuries. Rather unexpectedly, for such an intimate

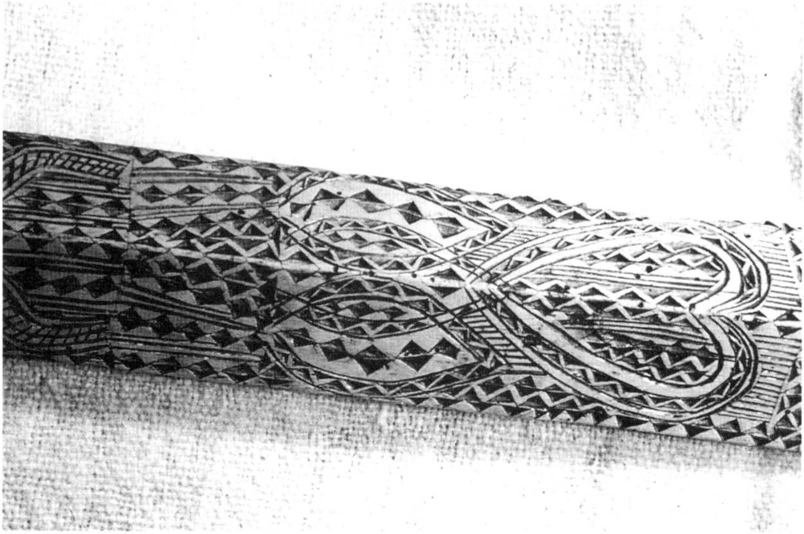

Detail of carving on a stay-busk.

(Welsh Folk Museum)

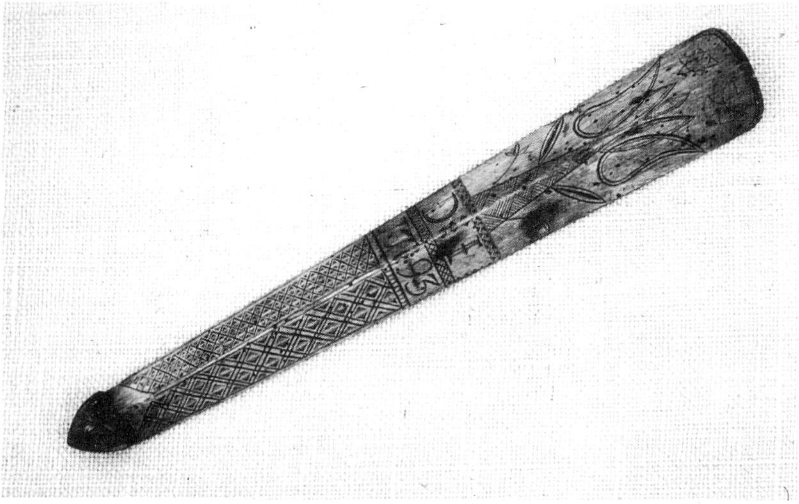

Stay busk

A piece of strong wood thrust down the middle of a stomacher to keep the stomach flat.

(Welsh Folk Museum)

object of fashion, carved stay busks also became tokens of love. Many were beautifully carved and the most common motifs were

> twin hearts and roundels, the remaining spaces being filled with love-birds, costume figures, flowers and leaf motifs, or geometric designs, varying from the coarse and simple, to finely chip-carved intricacies.[13]

The specimens that have reached the Welsh Folk Collection belong to the eighteenth century and come from the old counties of Radnor and Glamorgan. On one example there is a rare Welsh inscription declaring the lover's desperate plight *Wyf claf, wyf glew; clyw, gwel fi gwen* (I am love sick, I am valiant, hear, see me fair one or Gwen).[14] Another stay busk, dated 1768, bears the English words,'This bosk once had a heart'.[15]

Apple scoops, to help those with poor teeth to eat raw apples and to pull out apple cores, were also presented as love tokens.

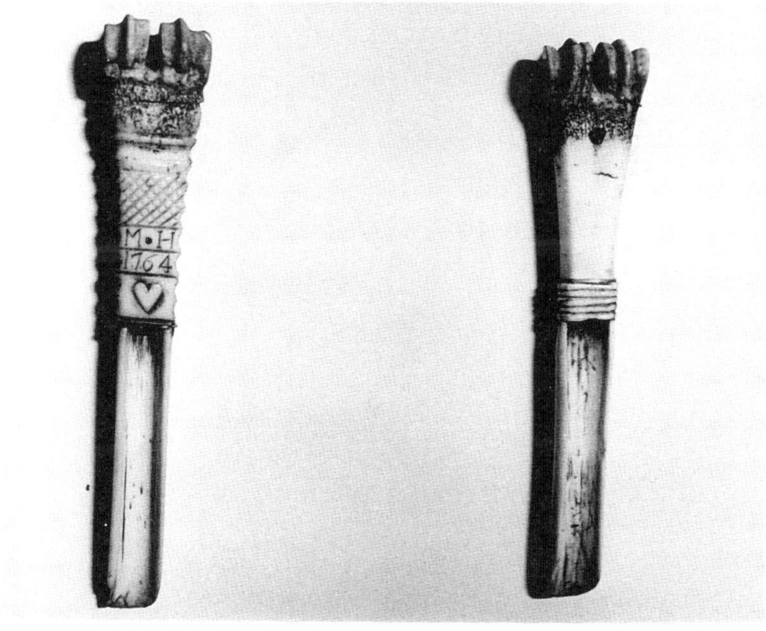

Apple scoops.

(Welsh Folk Museum)

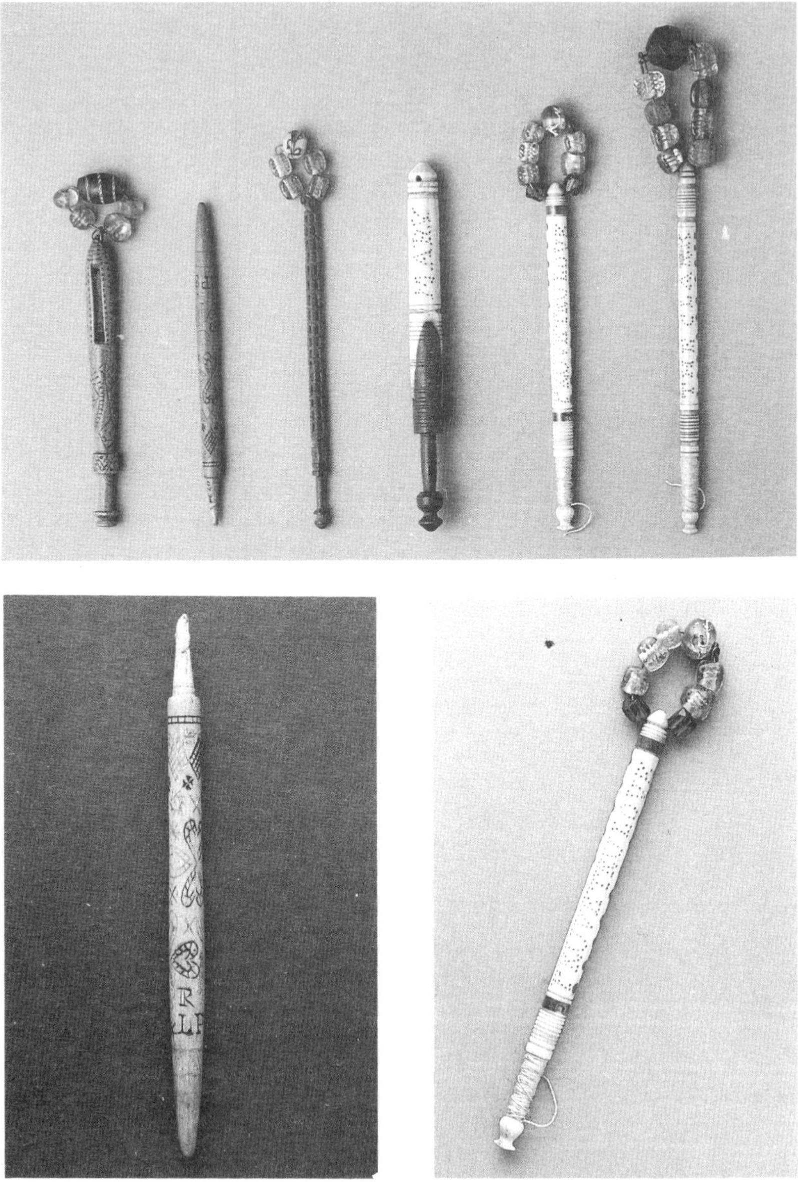

Lace bobbins.

(Welsh Folk Museum)

This custom can be traced back to Roman times, although most of the ones that have been preserved in the Welsh Folk Museum's collection date from the eighteenth and nineteenth centuries. Apple scoops would be carved from a sheep's leg bone and were often crudely decorated with initials, hearts, dates and other relevant motifs. Ivory and silver examples have also survived.[16] Several other everyday objects would be considered acceptable as love tokens. Young lads could make biscuit cutters, glove hooks or lace bobbins (purposefully and attractively turned from wood or bone) for their sweethearts, while the girls might choose to make pin cushions or book-marks to return their boyfriends' affection. Occasionally, a lover might seek a more individual gift. One admirer from the Aberystwyth area spent long hours carving intricate patterns on a cow-horn as a gift for his sweetheart in 1758,[17] while Hezekiah Thomas, a blacksmith from Lôn-las near Swansea, made a poker on behalf of his son Abraham Hezekiah Thomas to present to Hannah Maddock before they were married on 31 May 1870.[18]

During the long winter months young men would also derive much pleasure from trying to *clymu cwlwm cariad* (tie a lover's knot).[19] In Glamorgan these 'true lover's knots' were distributed as favours on St Valentine's Day and were often sent anonymously:

> great was the amusement and sometimes the consternation, of the youths and maidens when these favours appeared on the bodice or coat of anybody present at the revels often held on this day.[20]

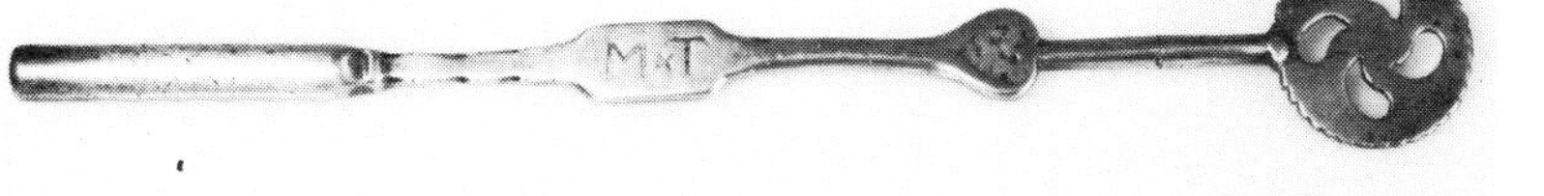

A poker made by the blacksmith Hezekiah Thomas from Lôn-las, Swansea, on behalf of his son to give to his sweetheart Hannah Maddock, 1870.
(Welsh Folk Museum)

The lover's knot was an intricate, intertwined pattern symbolizing everlasting love, and it was also often seen carved on the objects discussed above and on Valentine cards.

According to Pinto in his discussion of 'Small Woodware', love tokens such as these were considered merely as

> PRELUDES to courtship, not equivalents of engagement rings, and they were offered by the man as a sign that courtship was desired; consequently a village belle, were she a coquette, might accept a spoon from diverse would-be suitors.[21]

Yet this interpretation of the custom would seem to trivialize the tokens unnecessarily, especially when one considers the immense amount of labour and meticulous attention to detail which is displayed in so many of these seemingly trifling objects. Unfortunately, there is hardly any documentary evidence to prove what happened between lovers who had exchanged such love gifts, but for the few examples that have been recorded, such as the poker from Lôn-las and the love-spoon from Maentwrog, the tokens paved the way to marriage. Although it would be presumptuous to attribute to them the binding significance of engagement rings they were, undisputedly, sincere personal expressions of true and lasting devotion.

Gifts which do seem to have been exchanged in a lighter vein, and with no definite strings attached, were the ones sent to celebrate St Valentine's Day. It seems that the valentine in its earlier form was a person not a greeting as we know of it today (see further, Chapter 8) and that it was common for the admirer to send a gift to his chosen valentine. These gifts would not have been carved objects of wood but usually ready-bought tokens of love. A seventeenth-century Welsh poet, Edward Morris, Perthillwydion, wrote a poem to thank his loved one for a gift received on St Valentine's Day:

> *A gweddus yw imi, roi diolch amdani,*
> *I chwi, y fun heini, fwyn hynod.*[22]

(And it is meet that I thank you, remarkable, lively sweet maiden, for it.)

He does not specify the nature of the gift, but gloves and handkerchieves were very popular. The diarist, Samuel Pepys, during the same period, mentions the 'half a dozen pairs of gloves and a pair of silk stockings and garters' which his wife received from her valentine, Sir William Batten, in 1660.[23] According to the verses of another valentine, one could request a gift as well as give thanks for one. In one of the few Welsh valentine verses to have survived, the sender, Mary of Llanbryn-Mair, Montgomeryshire, reminds her admirer that she would like a gift:

nid wyf yn rhoddi arnoch Dasg
ond i chwi nghofio o hyn i'r pasg
a macin sidan cyfan coch
nei Bar o fenig yr in y fynoch.[24]

(I am not setting you a Task, but that you should remember me between now and eastertime with a complete red silk handkerchief or a pair of gloves—whichever you choose.)

By the nineteenth century the gift would be sent to accompany a valentine card, as the example received in 1845 from the Bridgend area, containing the message 'My dearest Sarah please to accept of this pair of gloves from your true lover' inside the card, suggests.[25]

A pair of gloves was also an acceptable gift to send to console a young maiden suffering from heartache. In one traditional Welsh folk-song the lover sends love-messengers to his dearest and promises to give her all he can afford:

Yr eos a'r glan hedydd
Ac adar man y mynydd
A ewch chi'n gennad at liw'r haf,
Sy'n glaf o glefyd newydd?

Does gennyf ddim anrhegion,
Na jewels drud i'w danfon,
I ddwyn i'ch cof yr hwn a'ch car,
Ond par o fenyg gwynion.[26]

(The nightingale and the fair skylark And the small mountain birds, Will you go as messengers to the bright coloured one Who is (love) sick from a new disease?

I have no presents, No expensive jewels to send, To remind you of the one who loves you Only a pair of white gloves.)

The same pattern can be seen in the custom of giving a piece of jewellery as a gift on St Valentine's Day. Before valentine cards became popular a wooer might send a ring or a brooch to his chosen valentine.[27] Once again, Samuel Pepys refers to this custom and, in doing so, shows that he mixed with the aristocracy. One of his acquaintances, a Miss Smart, must have been very much in demand, for

> The Duke of York, being once her valentine, did give her a jewel of about eight hundred pounds, and my Lord Mandeville, her valentine this year, a ring of about three hundred pounds.[28]

It is significant that several of the inscriptions quoted, associated with love tokens, contain references to heartache, lovesickness or a wounded heart. Perhaps the gift was seen as a means of restoring the former relationship. The rings given as valentine gifts were not considered to symbolize any form of binding contract as the engagement ring does today.

Other items of jewellery would make attractive love tokens too. The medieval poets mention *caeau* (brooches) and rings as love tokens and wrote *cywyddau*, strict metre verse, to thank their admirers for their generosity.[29] By the second half of the nineteenth century gold and silver brooches were in demand. They were not very expensive and the variety of designs offered plenty of choice. Some displayed the girlfriend's name, others bore sentimental inscriptions such as 'Forget me not' or 'Remember me' and Welsh examples can also be found. The word 'MIZPAH' was frequently engraved on brooches and lockets and worn by lovers who were likely to be separated for some time whether by a long sea voyage or some other extenuating circumstance. The inscription 'Mizpah' refers to the verse from the Book of Genesis (31: 49), 'And Mizpah; for he said, The Lord watch between me and thee, when we are absent one from another'. These items of jewellery would be inscribed with all kinds of love symbols; entwined hands, flowers, anchors, true lover's knots and hearts, of course.

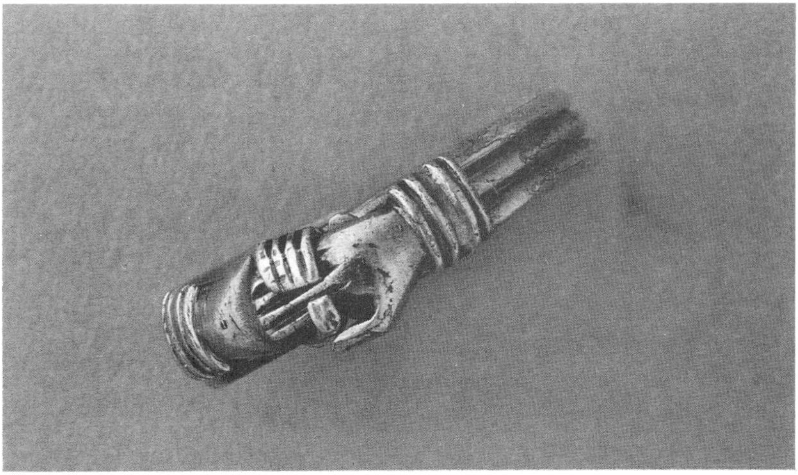

A ring showing hands entwined.
(Welsh Folk Museum)

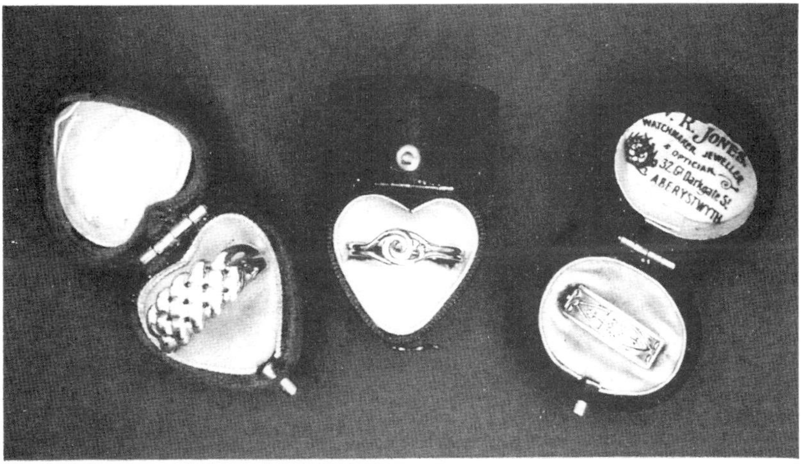

Three gold rings in their original boxes. From left to right:

(i) a keeper received by Mrs Jones, Bwlch-y-ddwyallt on her wedding day.
(ii) a ring depicting a true lover's knot c. 1850.
(iii) an engagement ring c. 1897. The decorative centre piece lifts to reveal the words 'Ever True'.

Gwen Davies's collection (from Taliesin, Dyfed)
(Welsh Folk Museum)

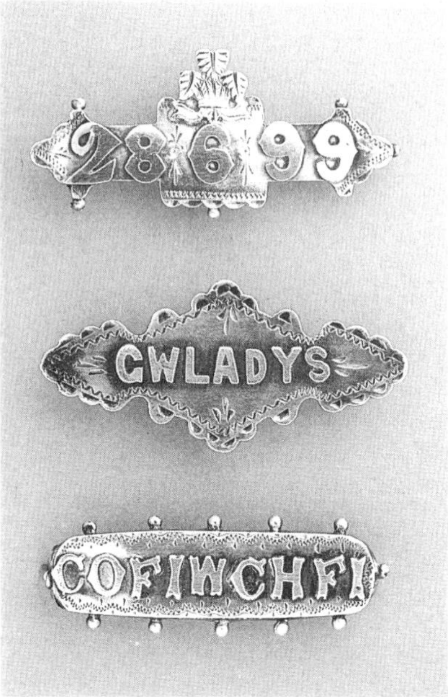

Silver brooches—especially popular as love tokens during the First World War.

The top one features a soldier's number, the middle one the sweetheart's name and the bottom one the sentiment 'Remember Me'.

(Welsh Folk Museum)

Love-bird brooches in jet mosaic.
Gwen Davies's collection (from Taliesin, Dyfed)
(Welsh Folk Museum)

Brooches given by sailors to their wives or sweethearts. Captain James Griffiths gave the anchor-shaped brooch to his girlfriend Jane Edwards, Clarach, Aberystwyth c. 1875. They married later.
Gwen Davies's collection (from Taliesin, Dyfed)

(Welsh Folk Museum)

Silver name brooches popular early in the twentieth century.

(Welsh Folk Museum)

(Welsh Folk Museum)

A Mizpah brooch. The inscription is derived from the Book of Genesis 31, 49, 'And Mizpah: for he said, The Lord watch between me and thee, when we are absent one from another.'

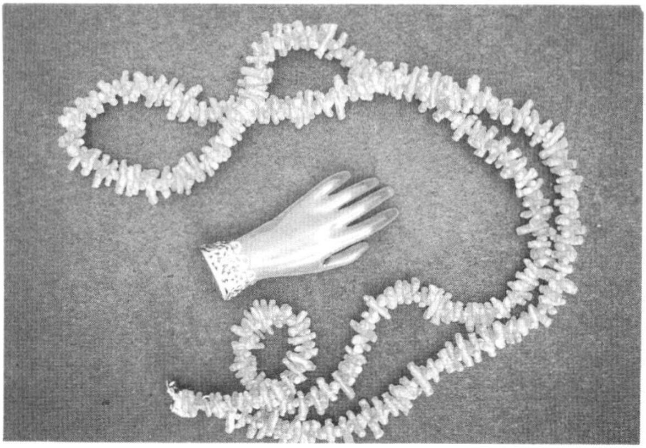

A coral necklace and brooch. It was maintained that this stone changed colour according to the wearer's health. Coral denoted true love. A left-hand coral brooch was said to be luckier than a right-hand one.
Gwen Davies's collection (from Taliesin, Dyfed)
(Welsh Folk Museum)

A necklace with a brooch attached to it. The brooch is a piece of coal set in a silver and glass frame. Coal miners used to send the first piece of coal they cut down a coal mine home to their wives or sweethearts.
Gwen Davies's collection
(from Taliesin, Dyfed)
(Welsh Folk Museum)

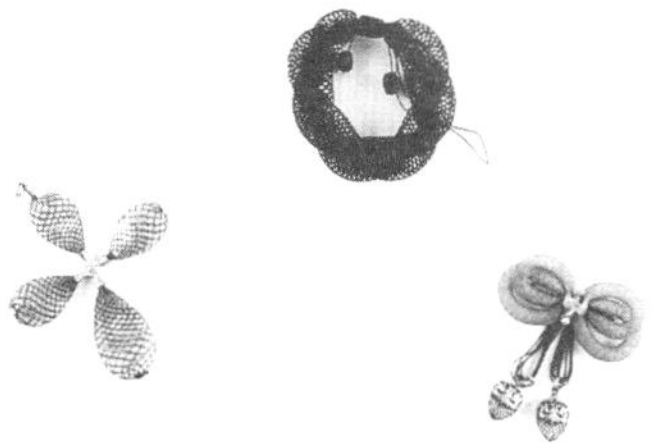

Brooches made from a sweetheart's hair.
(Welsh Folk Museum)

Lovers would often exchange locks of their hair and a girl might keep such a treasure in a locket or brooch. Lockets could also be used to hold a picture of one's beloved once the art of photography had developed sufficiently during the nineteenth century. Such gifts were not always welcome as these verses by Isaac Jones, a rhymester from Uwchaled, Denbighshire, illustrate. He had obviously received a picture of an admirer, Mary of Corwen, and was not too enamoured with the gift:

Ni fuasai'n rhaid it yrru
Dy lun ar bapur wedi'i dynnu,
Gan fy mod i'n gwybod gystled
Nad oedd yr un i'w chael gyn hylled.

Gwell gen i yw cael fy ngalw
'N gi cynddeiriog, daliwch sylw,
Neu'n beth hylla' dan yr wybren,
Nag yn gariad Meri o Gorwen.[30]

(You did not have to send Your photograph Since I knew full well That there was no one else as ugly as you. I would prefer to be called A mad dog, please note, Or the ugliest thing under the sun, Than Meri of Corwen's sweetheart.)

John Ceiriog Hughes, the well-known Victorian poet from Llanarmon Dyffryn Ceiriog in the same county, received a photograph of a sweetheart called Catrin, but he also rejected the gift and returned it accompanied, very callously, by a *Falanten Hyll* (an Ugly valentine):

Rwyn diolch am eich darlun
Y mae'n ddarlun da;
Rwyf wedi tori'm hesgyrn
Efo Ha! Ha! Ha!

Pwy wnaeth eich darlun, Catrin -
Darlun mor dda?
Mae'n werth y byd o chwerthin,
O Ha! Ha! Ha![31]

(I thank you for your picture It is a good one. I've split my sides with Ha! Ha! Ha! Who took your picture, Catrin,Such a good picture? It's worth the world in laughter, Oh Ha! Ha! Ha!)

Hatpins would also be most accceptable and appreciated as love tokens. During the First World War a young soldier out in the trenches would send home a button from his military dress. The young girl would have this made into the top of a hatpin and displayed it with great pride for all to see.[32] All manner of other objects could also serve as love tokens. Glass rolling pins, hair combs, decorative china, sugar tongs, and even bed-smoothers were presented by young admirers to their sweethearts, while in Caernarfonshire the greatest compliment a lover could pay to the girl he wished to woo would be to give her the first egg a young pullet laid![33]

Although it has been stressed that love-spoons and other intricate love tokens were not exchanged lightly between courting couples, it has also been noted that none of these tokens served as binding contracts or oaths of faithfulness and therefore equivalent in status to today's engagement ring. Yet one ritual was observed which was considered as a pledge between two lovers. It was customary, at least from the sixteenth century, for sweethearts to exchange coins which had been bent or 'bowed' to an angle of ninety degrees. As small coins, prior to the midseventeenth century, were not as thick as they are today, this task did not require Herculean strength. These bowed coins would be pierced, suspended from a ribbon and worn around the neck. When distance parted sweethearts for long periods the coin could be split in half and a piece retained by each party as a talisman. From the end of the eighteenth century these coins were engraved with initials, names or fanciful designs and were occasionally given as valentines. Yet they were usually taken very seriously and the contract they sealed between the couple was considered meaningful and to be honoured. The *Exeter Garland* of about 1750 noted a version of this custom using a ring:

> A ring of pure gold she from her finger took,
> And just in the middle the same then she broke,
> Quoth she, as a token of love you this take.
> And this as a pledge I will keep for your sake.[34]

A coin would be split in half in the Welsh version of the custom, recorded in both north and south Wales. In Montgomeryshire, the half coin would be worn 'secretly round the neck', suggesting that the betrothal was a private, rather than a public affair. Also

> if the pair remained true to one another the half coin was kept, but if they 'fell out' the half was either returned or thrown away.[35]

This was the case in the Neath Valley also, according to an essay presented at the Swansea National Eisteddfod in 1907. The coin commonly chosen was the threepenny piece, and if the courtship came to an end, the half coin had to be returned immediately. Indeed, if this was not done, awful consequences would surely overtake the unfaithful party:

> M G was courting a young man who was a mason, and a threepenny piece was broken in the usual way, but the young girl became ill and languished as a result of consumption. Mari fell in love with Rhys— and married him without returning her portion of the threepenny piece in her possession. One night, something seized her and took her out of bed and through the bedroom window. She remained out through the night until the morning, and when she returned her clothes were very muddy. This woman lived for years after this but could not look anybody in the face.[36]

Today's engagement ring probably derived from this older custom, although its exact origins are difficult to trace. It seems certain, however, that the ritual of engagement became increasingly popular during the intense upheaval of the First World War, and developed not only the engagement ring but all the elaborate commercial trimmings of the newspaper announcement, the engagement party and the accompanying gifts. All this seems worlds away from the patiently hand-carved and privately exchanged homemade traditional tokens of love.

NOTES

[1]*Cambro-Briton* iii, pp.36-7.
[2]Gillis, p.31.
[3]Macfarlane, pp.300-301.
[4]*The Shorter Oxford English Dictionary,* (1933), vol.ii.
[5]For the best treatment on the love-spoon see *W.F.C.*, pp.147-150.
[6]Baker, p.16.
[7]*Y Cymro,* 15/12/1981.
[8]W.F.M. Mss 1793/329, Evan Jones, Tynypant, Llanwrtyd.
[9]*Eisteddfod Gadeiriol Frenhinol Caerdydd, 1899, Rhestr o'r Testynau,* p.52.
[10]Trefor Owen (edit.), *The Story of the Lovespoon,* (Swansea, 1973), p.90.
[11]S Minwel Tibbott, 'Knitting Stockings in Wales—A Domestic Craft', *Folk-Life,* vol.xvi, 1978, p.65.
[12]Norah Waugh, *Corsets and Crinolines,* (London, 1954), p.150.
[13]Edward H Pinto, *Treen and other Wooden Bygones,* (London, 1968), p.22.
[14]W.F.M. 63.479/2.
[15]W.F.M. 63.479/1.
[16]Pinto, p.82.
[17]W.F.M. 64.503/1.
[18]Oral testimony Dr J Lewis, Glasfryn, 100 Frederick Place, Llansamlet, Swansea.
[19]Williams, p.351.
[20]Trevelyan, p.245.
[21]Edward H Pinto, *Treen or Small Woodware,* (London, 1949), p.34.
[22]Hugh Hughes, *Barddoniaeth Edward Morris, Perthi Llwydion,* (Liverpool, 1902), p.49.
[23]*W.F.C.*, p.154.
[24]W.F.M. 33.335/1.
[25]W.F.M. 46.132/2.
[26]W.F.M. Tape 4468, Mrs Buddug Lloyd Roberts, Cricieth.
[27]*W.F.C.*, First Edit. 1959, p.209, No. 254, 46.132/3.
[28]William Jones, *Finger-Ring Lore*, (London 1877), p.422.
[29]*GDG*, 84, p.230, Lewis, Roberts, Williams, Lxxiii.
[30]Robin Gwyndaf Jones, 'Y Cwlwm sy'n Creu' *Transactions of the Denbighshire Historical Society*, vol.xv, 1966, pp.208-9.
[31]*Gweithiau Ceiriog,* vol.i, 'Oriau'r Hwyr', (Wrexham, 1872), p.100.
[32]Mari Wynne Davies, 'Pinnau Het', *Y Wawr*, Haf 1987, p.23.
[33]John Jones, (Myrddin Fardd), p.156.
[34]Baker, p.15.
[35]A Bailey Williams, p.119.
[36]Trefor M Owen, 'West Glamorgan Customs', *Folk Life*, vol.iii, 1965, p.49.

Chapter 8

The Language of Love

As we have seen, one of the features of traditional courtship customs was the role the go-between played in setting-up and promoting a relationship between lovers. Sometimes, the go-between would be a *gwas-caru,* courtship attendant; a *ceisiwr*, seeker; or a *llatai*, intermediary. Poets, however, could employ the services of a different kind of *llatai* (messenger) and Welsh poetry from medieval times to the present has exploited this rich vein of expression to the full.

Dafydd ap Gwilym, as might be expected with so many reputed sweethearts scattered so widely, had plenty of work for such love messengers. Birds, such as the eagle, the skylark, the seagull, the blackbird and the woodcock, with their direct line of flight, were the speediest and most effective messengers, but he also made use of the deer and the salmon to convey his messages of love. He directed the skylark to Gwynedd where 'a fair and talented maiden' lived and charged it not to return empty-handed:

A chais un o'i chusanau
Yman i'w ddwyn ym, neu ddau. [1]

(And ask her for one [or two] of her kisses To be brought to me here.)

In the poem calling upon the wind as *llatai*, one is reminded of the custom of *mynd i gnocio* (going a-knocking). At Morfudd's home in Uwch Aeron he urges the wind:

Cur y ddor, par egori
Cyn y dydd i'm cennad i. [2]

(Knock the door, make it open Before daybreak for my messenger.)

Dafydd ap Gwilym, however, in this kind of poem tends to become side-tracked, to concentrate more and more upon the *llatai* itself than upon its message of love, so that the poem develops into a song of praise to the virtues and beauty of the messenger.

An unknown contemporary of Dafydd chose the swan to deliver his declaration of love:

Gwrando f'achwyn, addfwyn wr,
Wrthyd, a bydd i'm nerthwr.
Merch fonheddig sy'n trigaw,
A gwawr dlos sy gar dy law.
Brysia dithau, gorau gwr.
Wyn ei gesail negeswr . . .
Cyrch yn araf ei stafell,
Cyfarch o'th ben i wen well,
Addef fy nolur iddi,
A maent yw fy amwynt i. [3]

(Hear my complaint to you, gentle one, And be my support.
A noble maiden with a fair complexion lives near you
Hurry, best one, Messenger with the white breast . . .
Approach her room slowly,Greet the fair one with your mouth
Confess to her my pain And how great is my affliction.)

Folk-songs also used this convention and called upon the help of *llateion* to carry messages of love from one to another; as in this lovely dialect version from Glamorgan:

Y deryn du pigfelyn
A eu di drostoi'n dal;
Oddi yma i Ynys Forgan
A disgyn ar y wal?

A dwed yn fwyn wrth Gwenno
Am ddod i mas yn bost
Fod ar ei chariad llawan
Want ei gwel'd yn dost. [4]

(Yellow-beaked blackbird Will you go jauntily on my behalf
From here to Ynys Forgan And descend on the bedpost?
And tell Gwenno gently To come out at once
That her merry lover Wants to see her desperately.)

And traditional Welsh verses also saw the beauty of the *llatai*'s role as a love messenger:

Mi fum yn crwydro glan mor heli
Gwelwn wylan wen liw'r lili
Ar y traeth yn sychu ei godrau,
Wedi eu gwlychu gan y tonnau.
Mi rois fy mhen i lawr i wylo,
Fe ddaeth yr wylan ataf yno;
Mi rois lythyr dan ei haden
I fyn'd at f'annwyl siriol seren. [5]

(I wandered the salty seashore I saw the white seagull, the colour of the lily On the beach drying its nether parts, Made wet by the waves. I lay my head down to weep The seagull came over to me; I placed the letter under its wing To be taken to my dear cheerful star.)

The use of the *llatai* convention has enriched Welsh poetry through the centuries. Indeed one daring and rebellious medieval poet (perhaps Dafydd ap Gwilym himself) parodied the convention by sending his genitals as messengers to his chosen one.[6] It seems sad that sending a *llatai* is no longer a fashionable theme, even with the authors of pop songs or lighter melodies, in the second half of the twentieth century.

In the traditional verse quoted above, the forlorn lover gives the seagull a love letter for his sweetheart. Exchanging love letters has always been a favourite pastime even in a period of almost total illiteracy amongst the core of the population. Some would seek the assistance of the few literate members of their society, the village priest or chapel minister to help them to express their innermost feelings, while others would struggle on in their own way, often producing the most bombastic and incomprehensible prose.[7] When Taliesin Hiraethog of Cerrig-ydrudion wrote to his sweetheart in 1871, he admitted humbly his inadequacy and lack of experience at such a task:

I am so unaccustomed to the work of writing to my female friends that I have no idea what to say. If I only knew what those in my position usually say, I would try to say the same.[8]

It is hardly surprising that Montgomeryshire lovers resorted to such books as *On the Art of Writing Love Letters*, and that the girls who received these tokens of love should treasure them so greatly. If a girl received love letters from more than one lover she would parcel them individually, tying her favourite admirer's bundle securely with a blue ribbon.[9]

Perhaps the most forthright Welsh love letter to have survived was the one sent by seventeen-year-old Hannah Griffiths of Bodwrdda, Aberdaron, to her sweetheart, Mr Griffith Jones of Felin-hen. In it she declared herself in love and offered to marry him forthwith!

> You have drawn my Affection so much that I cannot be happy unless I tell you of my thoughts, and tell you in a word that I have looked at you with such liking that I would like to live with you as long as I live, however long that might prove to be.[10]

This letter was originally written in Welsh and such examples are rare. Most Welsh lovers, although they spoke the language fluently, because they had little, if any, schooling in its written form, preferred to write in English, however inadequate their command of it might be. Thus the fourteen love letters unearthed at Hayscastle, Pembrokeshire, which tell the tale of Mary Williams's involvement with three different suitors during the last quarter of the nineteenth century, were written in broken English. The three admirers had had to leave rural Pembrokeshire in search of work in the flourishing south Wales coalfield. Their letters are pragmatic in tone, for they were intended to pave the way for courting sessions on their return, for the hay harvest, the October fairs or the Christmas period. Although brief and often crudely expressed, as has been shown, these letters do reflect their period and shed some light upon the love customs of the age.[11]

An ardent lover could carry his message of love on to the letter's envelope too if he knew 'The Language of Stamps'. According to this 'language' the position of a stamp on an envelope revealed a secret message. If it was placed in the bottom left-hand corner it read 'I will never forget you'; the bottom right-hand corner asked 'When are you coming to see me?' and if it was attached to the top left-hand corner it carried a sorry message 'I cannot be yours'! The stamp placed in its traditional position in the top right-hand corner would read 'Have you forgotten me?' and remind the recipient that an answer was due soon.[12]

The advice in the 'Language of Stamps' was printed on a postcard. Indeed, postcards carrying love messages became popular towards the end of the last century and the beginning of the present, as the custom of taking holidays and going for trips became established generally. An acquaintance chose one such postcard, 'A Welshman's Love letter from Johnny Jones to his cariad Mary Jane Jones, Shop Manclochog' as a holiday greeting from Milford Haven to two Aberaeron sisters in 1935, although the contents of the 'love letter' could not have been relevant for them. In this fictional love message Johnny Jones tries to persuade his girlfriend Mary to leave her village home and venture south to work with him at a drapery store in Pontypridd. She would, he felt, help disprove the old saying that shop girls made poor wives.[13] This card and similar ones must have been common at shops throughout south Wales, and were used perhaps as subtle propaganda to draw young girls away from their rural employment to work in shops and offices in the industrial south.

During this period also the comic seaside postcard with its diet of large-bottomed ladies and weedy men came into its own. A variant upon this was the 'spooning card', carrying a message of love, and some of these were produced specifically for the Welsh market. In the Welsh versions the favourite theme was of the brash, sophisticated Englishman propositioning a lovely Welsh maiden, dressed, of course, in full traditional Welsh costume. His question would be in English and her reply in Welsh would be that she did not understand or that she had no interest in him. In one example the foreign admirer asks the girl:

> Prithee, Pretty Maiden will you marry me?

only to receive a verbose rebuff:

> *Chwenychwn unigrwydd annherfynol 'nhytrach trigiannu 'nghwmpeini creadur o'ch bath chi!*[14]

> (I would choose everlasting loneliness rather than dwell in the company of a creature like you!)

A WELSHMAN'S LOVE-LETTER.

From JOHNNY JONES
TO HIS CARIAD
MARY JANE JONES,
SHOP MANGLOCHOG.

STAFF STREET,
PONTYPRIDD.

My Dear Mary Jane,

It was not for want of think that I did not wrote you a love-letter sooner and this cause I think of you every hour of the day and every day of the year, and I do love your father too, cause he did lend his horse and cart to brought me to the Station on Monday. Indeed of goodness I shall never forgot, to remember what you did tell me when coming in the cart. Oh! Mary Jane my darling stick to your promise won't you, my dear? I did rive in Pontypridd safe and sound and I did go strait to the shop and when the master did see me he did say to me "Man from where you are" and I did told him I was John from Manglochog coming to work in his shop, then he did knowed me in a minit look you, my work is selling cotton and tapes and hundreds of other little things, yes millions. they do call it the happy compartment or something, but indeed of goodness it is, not very happy at all to be here without you, the girl I do love better than nobody, for all the time I am thinking of you. Oh yes will you ask my mother for my watch if it is walking cause it will be very handy for me in the morning to know what o'clock it is she do know my directions. There is a lot of girls in the shop but not one to match you Mary Jane. How long are you going to stop in Mary Jones' Shop again Mary Jane? cause I will try and get you a job in Pontypridd to be a Millinder, I will ask Mr. Thomas the Draper about a vacancy to you for they say he do give good wages to his clerks and bye and bye we will marry, is it not my dear? They say shop girls do not make good wives but you know what Mr. Evans the Schoolmaster did say, put a rose wherever you like it will have the smell of a rose and put a donkey wherever you like it will be a donkey and like that you are my dear Mary Jane, I believe shop girls will make good wives if they only get the chance. Well I will not wrote you a bigger letter this time for if it was twice as big I could never told you how much I do love you. If you don't get this letter write back to me at once. I have send you a little bit of poetry I do make myself last night, I must finish now cause I can here someone asking for hooks and eyes and your dear loving John must go forward.

—JOHN.

Oh! Mary Jane my darling,
I love you in my heart,
I told you so last Monday,
When coming in the cart.

What if the horse did understand,
What I to you did say,
I have no doubt my darling,
He would have run away.

I always love you Mary Jane,
And you be true to me,
And come up soon to Pontypridd,
To sell some drapery

The[illegible]nd bye we will marry,
And enjoy our little lives,
The boy from Pontypridd shall see
If Shop Girls make good wives.

On another spooning card the English wooer presents his suit in verse but receives the same modest reply '*Dim Saesneg*!' (No English) each time:

While rambling alone on the moor yesterday,
I asked a nice girl if she would show me the way;
She blushed, was so shy, she could only reply—
'*Dim Saesneg*'

I asked her sweet name, if her mother was nigh,
I looked at her lovingly; heaved a great sigh,
Her smile was delicious, bewitching her cry,
'*Dim Saesneg*'

I drop on my knees, all my love songs recite;
I plead for her love, picture love's sweet delight:
But the Welsh girl replies as she laughs at the sight,
'*Dim Saesneg*'[15]

Spooning Card c. 1906-10.
(National Library of Wales)

"THE CYMRAEG GIRL"
Hello! Hello! Hello!
its a CYMRAEG GIRL this time
A CYMRAEG HAT, a CYMRAEG NOSE
CYMRAEG HAIR and CYMRAEG CLOTHES
Hello! Hello! Hello!
to me its very plain
I've tickled a Welsh CARIAD'S Fancy
So I've changed my girl again
The Welsh "CARIAD"
The Girl I left behind

(National Library of Wales)

HEN WLAD FY NHADAU.
(WALES.)
Dear
I wass be
enjoying myself
tip-top —
Lovely
Scenery!!

(National Library of Wales)

(National Library of Wales)

Spooning Cards c. 1906-10.

ABERYSTWYTH BAY.
Only wanse I was so fun-ny,
Hob y derry dan-do.
Court a 'oo-man with no mo-ney.
Dy-na gan-u et-to.
When she ask-ed me to marry,
Down, derry down.
No, you sha'nt be Mistress Parry.
Down, down, hei derry down
My darling Ma-ry do not frown,
Sian fwyn, tyr'd i'r llwyn,
My darling Ma-ry do not frown.

(National Library of Wales)

Welsh girls are portrayed as bewitching flirts on these spooning cards and they were intended, doubtlessly to attract visitors to the country. An Aberystwyth postcard, probably one version of a similar card popular at other seaside resorts, proclaimed that:

> Travel North, South, East and West,
> Aberystwyth girls are voted best.[16]

During the nineteenth century and up until the present day, the most popular of all love greetings were the cards exchanged between lovers on St Valentine's Day, 14 February. Yet the origins of the custom of celebrating this saint's feast day are obscure and have to be traced back into early Christian times. The Romans held the festival of Lupercalia, the god of fertility, on 14 February and during the gaieties young men would draw lots to decide who would be their partners for the day. As the Christian St Valentine was martyred upon this same date about the year AD 270, his name became linked with the older feast with its pagan rites and gradually absorbed some of its features. The feast developed in significance and

> Tempered by the pervasive influence of the medieval church and made respectable by the patronage of a saint, the custom survived in a changed form.[17]

Thus the early valentine was not a greeting or a card but a person. In a series of love letters from late medieval Norfolk, Margery Paston writes to her lover Richard Calle: 'upon Friday is Saint Valentine's Day, and every bride chooseth him [sic] a mate'.[18] This 'raffling' of lovers was common amongst 'The Vulgar' well into the eighteenth century as Bourne in his *Antiquitates Vulgares*, 1725, reveals, and once the lot had been drawn it was 'looked upon as a good omen' of their being man and wife afterwards.[19] By the seventeenth and eighteenth centuries, as we have seen (Chapter 7), it had become customary to give gifts or love tokens, gloves, rings, kerchiefs or true lover's knots to one's chosen valentine on this feast day. The earliest Welsh references prove that Welsh lovers also exchanged gifts. The poem by Edward Morris (1607-89) of Perthi-Llwydion to thank his sweetheart for a 'valentine gift' has already been noted but it also contains a feature found in several other valentine verses of this period. He plays with the word 'El' describing his sweetheart as 'Beautiful golden El, delightful El, pure white El; second only to Gloria' and one can tentatively suggest that El was the girl's name, or part of it, or even a pet name for her.[20] This was certainly a feature of a similar poem, written by an anonymous poet towards the beginning of the eighteenth century, by, or on behalf of, a young maiden to ask for a *falendein* (valentine). Her choice, if she were lucky enough *ei dynnu'n falendein* (to draw him as a valentine) would be her lover, Lewis Jones, and his name is interwoven into the fabric of the verse.[21]

Dafydd Jones of Trefriw (1708?-85) also incorporates the initials of his *falendein*'s name into the body of his poem and although the Christian name is difficult to decode, the surname seems to have been Foulk. He describes how he drew her name from amongst ten others to be his valentine:

> *I ac A, haulwen Ha, hoyw-wen serchog,*
> *Yw fy angyles enwog, E ac N, walches wen;*
> *Ac E dros ben, hawddgarwch byd;*
> *F, ac O drefnus dro, drwyadl ei 'madroddion,*
> *Lana erioed a welson, U, L, K, fowels dda,*
> *Galonnog o'r lawena i gyd:*
> *Eich enw chwi ddae i mi o ddeg,*
> *Yn Falendein ma'r ddalen deg.*[22]

(I and A, summer sunshine, affectionate lively one, Is my famous angel, E and N, fair noblewoman; And an E over, world's loveliness; F and O in order, through her speech, The fairest we ever saw, U, L, K, good vowels, Hearty, of the most cheerful: Your name has come to me out of ten As a Valentine here is the fair sheet of [lottery] paper.)

Although Huw Morys (1622-1709) does not name in anagrammatic form his sweetheart in his poem, he does mention his hope that he will be lucky in the draw and that he will have his choice as a *falendein*. Yet if chance does not favour him, he asks his loved one for some other token of love before May Eve and he promises:

Mi a'i gwisgaf bob dydd, tra bo'ch a'ch llaw'n rhydd.
I gofio'ch hawddgarwch, difyrwch a fydd.[23]

(I'll wear it every day, whilst you have your hand free,
To remind me of your loveliness, it will be a pleasure.)

Further references to drawing and choosing one's valentine occur even into the nineteenth century,[24] yet it must be remembered that although these poems name and mention valentines, they were not valentines themselves and were not accompanied by a card. The custom, as we know of it today, had not developed fully yet for it did not gain a proper footing until the end of the eighteenth century.

The first written valentine message in England dates from as early as 1684[25] while the oldest example of a handmade valentine card is dated 1750.[26] Some early Welsh examples of homemade valentines can be found among the Welsh Folk Museum's collection. One of these, if it can in fact be counted a valentine, is made in the form of a true lover's knot, one of the love tokens associated with 14 February, and its simplicity seems far removed from the later, Victorian models. The Arberth (Pembrokeshire) valentine, on the other hand is a genuine valentine card and displays a craft design typical of early valentine and Christmas greetings. To form the design, a piece of paper was folded symmetrically and then cut or torn to create a beautifully delicate doily style lacework. The greetings were written around these folds and patterns, and contained a verse expressing love and devotion.[27] A verse from the Welsh language, homemade valentine from Llanbryn-Mair, Montgomeryshire, has already been quoted as it referred to the exchanging of gloves and kerchiefs as love tokens. The sender also incorporates a traditional Welsh verse in his greeting and then seeks to justify this lack of originality:

fallai Dywedwch chwi am Danaf
mai hen Benillion sosi yrraf
Dyweid yn wir a allaf finai
mai hen ffasiwn iw ffalantai[28]

(Perhaps you will say of me That I send you saucy old verses, I can only truthfully reply That valentines are an old custom [or that Valentines are old fashioned].

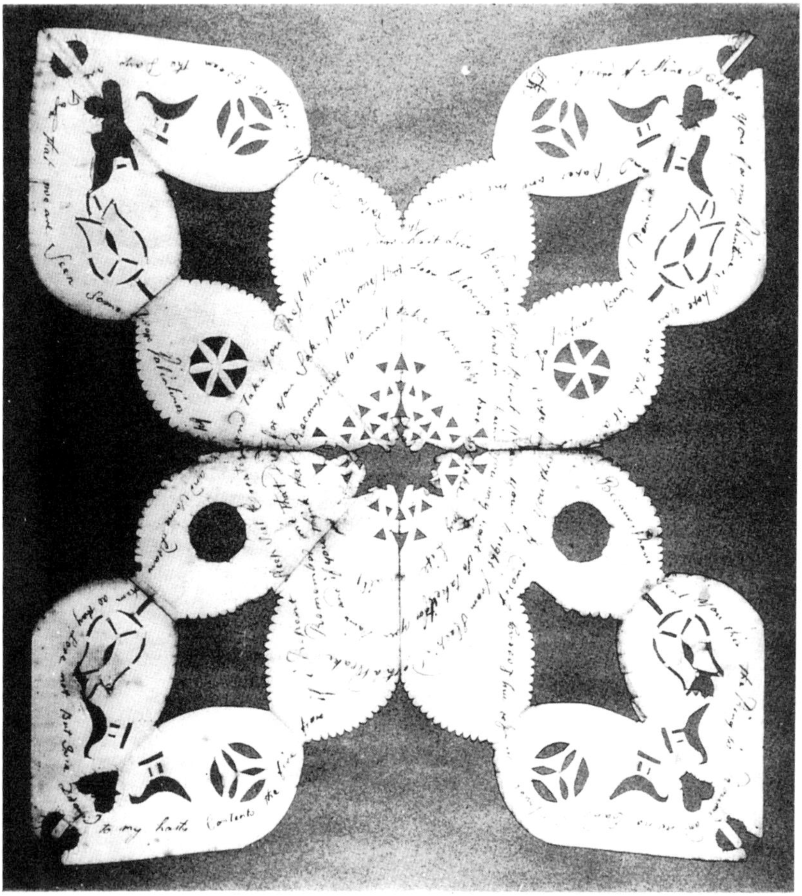

Arberth Valentine (homemade)

(Welsh Folk Museum)

Llanbryn-Mair Valentine (homemade)
(Welsh Folk Museum)

Llanderfel Valentine (homemade)
(Welsh Folk Museum)

The technique used in the Arberth valentine was also found on three early Edeyrnion, Merionethshire, examples and is probably an adaptation of the skill needed to carve similar intricate tracery patterns on love-spoons and other love tokens. The verses on the centre panels are in English, although the senders and recipients were probably monoglot Welsh speakers. They were, in fact, versions of the ones found in the *Valentine Writers*, published at the beginning of the nineteenth century. The poor spelling and inaccurate line-endings suggest that in this case the texts were not copied directly but written down from memory.[29]

Hopeful lovers in the Welsh border area could seek the assistance of two local valentine-makers, if they could afford the fee of half a crown. The earliest example of their work, according to a detailed description in *Bye-gones*, was dated 1826 while an 1885 example was 'probably made in extreme old age'! As with the Arberth and the Edeyrnion versions these men used the craft of paper folding and cutting to form intricate lacework patterns which they further decorated ornately:

The whole is surrounded by a border of painted hearts, in various stages of inflammation. In the corners are turtle doves of the same colour as parraquets and yellow finches, eating cherries as big as their own heads; loving couples in various loving attitudes; the swain in brown beaver stove-pipe hat, sky-blue swallow-tail coat, with gilt buttons, and yellow smalls; the maiden in scanty skirt of mousseline-de-laine, scarlet petisse and antiquated bonnet of straw, with a high crown and short poke—very convenient for kissing.[30]

Yet the demand for valentine greetings grew so rapidly during the nineteenth century, that the handmade variety became supplanted by the mass-produced factory cards. The individual lover could still stamp his own personality upon such a card if he chose by, perhaps, buying the uncoloured variety and colouring it himself, or more commonly, by composing a personal greeting or verse, or commissioning someone else to write one on his behalf. Traditional Welsh verses were popular with such lovers especially if they also contained the formula of the valentine as a *llatai* or love messenger:

Folant fach, O! cerdd yn fuan
Paid ag aros dim yn unman,
Disgyn lawr ar bost y gwely,
Lle mae nghariad fach i'n cysgu.

(Sweet Valentine Oh! go quickly. Do not tarry at all anywhere, Descend on the post of the bed Where my true love is sleeping.)

Another popular traditional valentine verse was:

Dyma'r folant wyf yn anfon
Attat ti o fodd fy nghalon,
Gan obeithio caiff roesawiad
Gyda thi, fy anwyl gariad.[31]

(This is the valentine I send To you, to my heart's delight, Hoping, my dear sweetheart, that you will welcome it.)

The Welsh form *folant* (or *ffolant/ffalant; molant/malant*) was, by the nineteenth century, gradually superceding the obviously borrowed version *falandein/falendein* from the English 'valentine', found in the earlier works.

Ardent admirers could also try commissioning country poets to write valentine greetings on their behalf. These country poets served their community well, by celebrating baptisms and marriages in verse, and writing long, commemorative poems in honour of the dead. Dewi Dyssul of Maslan was the main valentine composer of the Llandysul area and he would respond to each individual client's request and situation, as in this rather morbid example to be sent by a young maiden to Ifan Tomos:

Mi gara'r enw Ifan
Tra'r huan fry uwch ben
A'm gwaed yn taer ergydio
A gwallt yn cuddio mhen,
Ac yn fy oriau olaf
Bydd Ifan gen i'n gu
Ac wrth ei ochr carwn
Fod yn y ddaear ddu.

Y Folant hon ddanfonir
Gan ddifir feinir fwyn,
At Ifan Tomos lwysaidd
Fab c'ruaidd lawn o swyn;
Heb ynthi unrhyw weniaeth,
Trwm hiraeth garia'm bron,
O eisiau bod yn wastad
O hyd i'w chariad llon. [32]

(I shall love Ifan's name While the sun shines up above, While my blood continues to pump brightly And while there is hair on my head, And during my last hours Dear Ifan will be with me, And I would like to be at his side in the black earth.

This valentine is sent By a pleasant gentle maid To handsome Ifan Thomas, A loving youth, full of charm; It contains no flattery. Heavy longing stirs my breast Because I always want to be true to her [?] love.)

Another of Dewi Dyssul's valentines was intended to be sung to the ballad tune '*Gwel yr Adeilad*' which does prove that some of these poems, especially the traditional harp verses, would have been sung by the lover or his representative to his valentine. [33]

A Victorian valentine

(Welsh Folk Museum)

A Victorian valentine

(Welsh Folk Museum)

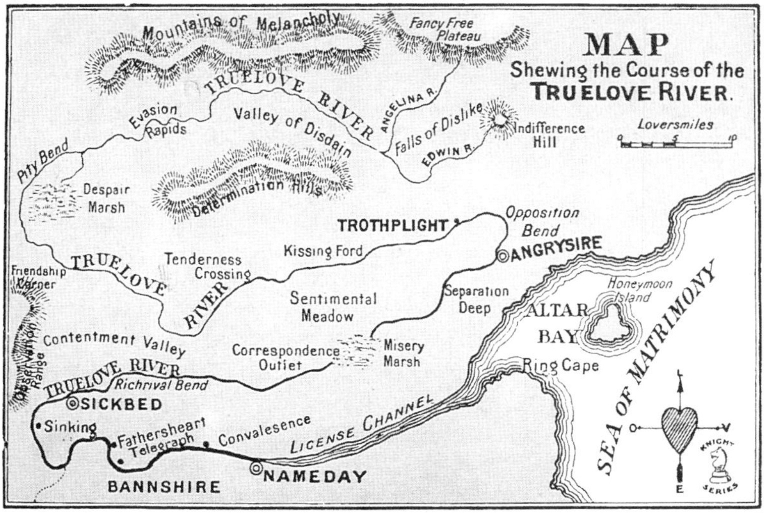

Map of True Love

(Welsh Folk Museum)

Trebor Mai, a Caernarfonshire poet (1830-77), wrote *englynion,* four-lined stanzas and *cywyddau*, strict metre verse as valentines on behalf of the young people of his locality[34] but the majority were similar to the examples already quoted from south Cardiganshire.

One verse from Llanwenog parish was directed towards the girl and refers to Cupid's live arrow. It reads as follows in translation:

> I haven't got a pound to spend on you Cati. I can only spare a HEART, Take it. An arrow has shot through it to the farthest end. As you see; You are the only one that can make it better—You have the cure.[35]

Two other valentine verses recorded in the nearby Rhydlewis area make use of the blackbird as a *llatai* to carry messages of love, one to Wern-ddu and the other to Dyffryn Cerdin, for the girl sending the valentine in each case is in a sorry plight.[36] In a later example from Felin-fach, the girl, or rhymester, recalls the saying that birds choose their mates on 14 February and it goes on to vow that if she were allowed to choose a partner from all the lads of Ceredigion (perhaps an echo of the lottery custom?) she would choose the recipient of the poem as her lover.[37]

Yet all valentines were not as pleasantly sentimental and attractive as these. During the nineteenth century the comic valentine came into fashion. It was

> a masterpiece of the grotesque, with barbed verse and unflattering colour, far from sentimental, expressing everything but love.[38]

The Welsh adopted this custom avidly, and two kinds of light valentines emerged, the *ffolant ysmala,* the comic valentine and the *ffolant salw*, the ugly valentine. The comic variety were harmlessly funny and could not have hurt the recipient as these two examples, both once again from south Cardiganshire, illustrate:

Dyma ffolant, ffolant lon,
Dim ond dimai roes am hon,
Os caiff hon fynd lan drwy'r simnai
Wfft i fi am roi y ddimai.

(Here is a valentine, cheery valentine. I only paid a halfpenny for it, If it is sent up the chimney [i.e. burnt] Woe unto me for wasting a halfpenny.)

Y mor a gilia o Gwmtydu
A'r Foel a droir a'i baglau fyny
Twm Brynhyfryd droir yn ynad
Neu yn llywydd gwlad y lleuad
Neu yntau'r lleuad droir yn llo
Cyn byth anghofia i nghariad[39]

(The sea will have retreated from Cwmtydu And the Foel will have been turned upside down Twm Brynhyfryd will have been made a magistrate Or president of the Land of the Moon Or the moon will have been turned into a calf Before I ever forget my dearest love.)

Perhaps, after all, this last valentine was not really intended to be a comic valentine at all, but that the rhymester had run out of poetic muse!

The *ffolantau salw*, or ugly valentines, were more difficult to digest and would certainly have offended the recipient. The

Llanwenog example was directed very personally at one Tomos who obviously took little pride in his appearance:

Mae'r folant yma'n dangos
  Shwt fachan wyti, Tomos;
Pwy all roi cusan fyth ar swch
  Sy'n fwrfwch fel yr andros.

Mi rown lapswchad iti
  Pe gwisget shilcen deidi,
A britsh benlin a gwasgod flot
  A cot fel Ianto Cati[40]

(This valentine shows What kind of a lad you are, Tomos; Whoever could kiss lips Which are so terribly hairy? I would give you a long kiss If you wore a tidy jerkin and knee breeches and a waistcoat And a coat like Ianto Cati.)

Young men could be equally unchivalrous towards maidens who thrust themselves upon them, as in this ugly valentine which reads in translation:

I have a sweetheart in the mill who has wild boar's teeth, and pig's eyes, and two feet similar to a swan's. She speaks like an owl.[41]

This last example was, once more, recorded in Cardiganshire. But, although no Welsh ugly valentines have survived from the rest of Wales, we can be fairly sure that they were popular generally. Perhaps valentine senders from other parts of Wales bought one of the many commercially produced English versions that were flooding the market in late Victorian times. Many of these, often grotesque comic valentines, have survived in the Welsh Folk Museum's collection. One example bears the picture of a woman carrying a large parasol. Her skirts lift up to reveal a circular frame, her underclothes and this uncomplimentary verse:

Ears like Donkey, Eyes like cat,
To be genteel, you are too fat
While there's another in the land
I'll never claim your mutton hand.[42]

Grotesque, funny or satirical valentines.

London: Marks & Sons.

DAIRY MAID.

Oh Dolly, Dearest Dairy Maid,
To wed you I would be afraid,
But there you're giving such a leer,
It almost churns my heart my dear.
To see you churning at that churn,
And legs with such a graceful turn,
I'm sure my dear, my heart you'd win.
But still you're rather short of tin.

(Welsh Folk Museum)

Yes you can spout and you can preach,
But what does all your talking teach.
We know as much when you have done,
As when you that long speech begun.

(Welsh Folk Museum)

Your meanness is known to the whole
country round –
The barber I'm sure won't defend it;
You've got a big store of small coin I'll
be bound.
Why don't you stop hoarding and
spend it?

(Welsh Folk Museum)

NOVELETTE
You always say you're fond of kids,
I'm much inclined to doubt;
I think your worship is for quids,
Which mostly you're without.

(Welsh Folk Museum)

The artistic development of the valentine card, from the handmade early examples to the ornate and elaborate designs of the mid Victorian period, has been traced in detail by Ruth Webb Lee in her excellently illustrated study of the subject.[43] The details need not be repeated here as the factory-made valentines sent in Wales did not differ in this respect from their English counterparts. It was the Welsh verses, often homespun and basic in form and content which gave Welsh valentines their special flavour, and that is why examples have been so widely quoted here.

The introduction of the Penny Post in 1840 gave the valentine industry a new fillip and the custom became increasingly popular during the next half century. According to the GPO's figures, 800,000 valentines were posted in 1855, but the figure had risen to 1,634,000 in 1880.[44] This trend was reflected in Wales:

> In Cardiff the postmaster thinks himself lucky if he gets off with 15,000 letters in excess of the ordinary mail. Nineteen extra sorters and carriers were employed for the work on February 14th 1878, and the regular force was heavily worked beyond its usual hours.[45]

According to the Llanwenog parish historians, writing of the practice in 1939, the custom of sending valentines had declined rapidly during the decade between 1880 and 1890 but seemed to be reviving during the period of writing.[46] Other sources do not substantiate this theory, although there does seem to have been a strong tide of anti-valentine feeling in that part of south-west Wales during these years. An entry under the village of Dinas on 26 February, 1881 in *The Dewsland and Kemes Guardian*, reflects this view. The correspondent writes:

> We last year called attention to . . . the practice . . . of pestering people with valentines, full of slanderous abuse and obscene insinuations which would bring a blush to the cheek of any virtuous man and woman. This, we are sorry to say, has been indulged in to a greater extent than ever this month, and we would respectfully call the attention of the ministers of all religious bodies to this degrading habit.

He goes on the describe how one opponent of the custom symbolically set fire to a valentine in the village Post Office as a mark of his disapproval![47]

In spite of such attitudes, the custom did survive into the twentieth century, although, as with so many other folk customs, it went through fluctuating periods. Myrddin Fardd testifies that 'hundreds and thousands of notes' were posted in Caernarfonshire on St Valentine's Day during the first decade, and Kate Davies, a native of Pren-gwyn, Llandysul, could recall the importance of the practice during the same period. She could remember how the boys would be willing to pay two shillings or half a crown for a good valentine, and that many were trimmed with silk threads and flowers and packed attractively into boxes. The girls who received these love greetings would treasure them and display their favourites on the dresser after they had married.[49] Valentines are still exchanged between lovers today, of course, some with a true and intense feeling of love, others sent in a lighter vein, but the practice has become totally commercialized and has lost most of its meaning as a folk custom.

Other miscellaneous traditions and beliefs have been associated with St Valentine's Day too:

> Dreams of St Valentine's Eve were supposed to be fateful. A child born on Valentine's Day would have many lovers. The farmers said a calf born on St Valentine's Day was of no use for breeding purposes. If hens were set to hatch on St Valentine's Day all the eggs would be rotten.[50]

All these associated customs and beliefs serve to illustrate how important St Valentine's Day was in the traditional folk calendar. As the feast day fell in mid-winter when spirits were low, and yet when everyone was anticipating the romantic stirrings of spring, the celebration of the patron saint of lovers' festival gave young people a chance to relieve tensions, and forget, for a day, the monotonous round of daily life.

Yet, while acknowledging fully the significance of St Valentine's feast day, it would be remiss, in a book on Welsh love customs, not to recognize the importance of Wales's own patron saint of lovers, St Dwynwen. According to tradition,

Dwynwen was one of Brychan Brycheiniog's twenty-four children and lived during the fifth century. Her history is obscure but Iolo Morgannwg, the remarkable eighteenth-century forger and romantic, relates a strange tale to explain how she became accepted as the patron saint of Welsh lovers. According to Iolo Dwynwen fell in love with a youth called Maelon Dafodrill, who returned her affection with passion. Indeed, he tried to seduce her before their betrothal, but she refused. He, in return, cast aspersions on her and caused Dwynwen extreme distress. In her anguish she prayed for God's intervention, that she could be relieved of her love for Maelon. God appeared to her in a dream and offered her a sweet potion to drink. She was immediately released of her heartache. Maelon was given the same potion but he was turned by it into a block of ice. Then God granted Dwynwen three wishes: she asked for Maelon to be set free from his icy prison; that she should live celibately and never marry for the rest of her days; and that she could assume the role of interceder between lovers. The three wishes were fulfilled and Dwynwen became a saint and nun, and later the patron saint of Welsh lovers.[51]

Her cult spread the length and breadth of Wales. In Glamorgan, it accumulated strange traditions:

> Dwynwen's symbol was the crescent moon; her magical girdle had the same attributes as the Cestus of Venus, and she carried a bow of destiny. During her last visit to earth she left her bow on the yellow sands of her southern shrine, wherefrom it was seized and turned into stone by the Hag of the Night, who fixed it about ten feet below the roof of Tresillian Cave, Glamorgan, where it is still to be seen. It is customary in the present day for people to visit this cave to try their luck under the bow of destiny. The trial consists of flinging a pebble over the natural arch of stone. If successful the first time, the person will be married within the current year. Each failure represents one year of life. In South Wales, on the shore of the Severn Sea, the festival of Dwynwen was held in April, when, it is asserted, she last visited the earth and left in her footprints the blossoms of spring.[52]

It was to Llanddwyn and Porthddwyn on Anglesey, however, that pilgrims flocked during the Middle Ages to commemmorate St Dwynwen. Her feast day was celebrated on 25 January. The

Remains of the church at Llanddwyn, centre of the St. Dwynwen cult, as patron saint of lovers.

(Marian Delyth)

rectory at Llanddwyn came under the auspices of Bangor Cathedral and the substantial income derived from the pilgrim's offerings greatly subsidized the cathedral's income.[53] The pilgrims came to seek the assistance of the patron saint of Welsh lovers mainly in matters of the heart. As might be expected, Dafydd ap Gwilym, that great fourteenth-century love poet, travelled to Llanddwyn, where he describes the 'brightly-lit choir' and the 'golden image' of the saint in the church. He requested Dwynwen to go as a *llatai* or love-messenger on his behalf to his beloved Morfudd, and also asked her to release him from this cruel heartache:

Gwna fi'n iach, weddusach wawd,
O'm anwychder a'm nychdawd . . .
Eiriol, er dy greuol gred
Ar em Wyry roi ymwared.[54]

(Cure me, praise would be finer, of my indisposition and feebleness . . . Call upon, for the sake of your blood-stained belief, Your treasured Virgin to deliver me.)

It is typical of Dafydd's audacity that he dares to invoke chaste Dwynwen's support in his clandestine relationship with Morfudd, a married woman.

An anonymous poet of the same period relates how he, also, had been rejected in love and how he had promised himself a visit to Llanddwyn to seek a cure for his lovesickness.[55] Syr Dafydd Trefor, a late medieval poet-priest from Caernarfonshire, concentrated, as befitted a man in holy orders, upon describing Dwynwen's shrine in his poem. He praises her statue, her sanctuary and the miracles wrought at her holy wells. Love-torn pilgrims came 'like a King's armies', bearing candles and large offerings.[56] These offerings provided Rhisiart Cyffin, who was Black Dean of Bangor from *c.*1480-1502 with sufficient income to build himself a fine house at Llanddwyn.[57] Cyffin also rebuilt the choir of Bangor Cathedral, during his period as dean, and incorporated into the choir a window depicting St Dwynwen, among other saints.[58]

St Dwynwen's Well attracted lovers from far and wide, too. It was reputed to be inhabited by a sacred eel or fish, whose movements indicated the fortunes of the lovesick people who resorted to it. An account of the ritual was written by William Williams of Llandygái, *c.*1800:

> There was a spring of clear water, now choked up by the sand, at which an old woman from Newborough always attended, and prognosticated the lovers' success from the movements of some small eels which waved out of the sides of the well, on spreading the lover's handkerchief on the surface of the water. I remember an old woman saying that when she was a girl, she consulted the woman at this well about her destiny with respect to her husband; on spreading her handkerchief, out popped an eel from the north side of the well, and soon after another crawled from the south side, and they both met on the bottom of the well; then the woman told her that her husband would be a stranger from the southern part of Caernarfonshire. Soon after, it happened that three brothers came from that part and settled in the neighbourhood, . . . one of whom . . . in a little time, married her. So much of the prophecy I remember. This couple was my father and mother.[59]

Since the Middle Ages, as this passage indicates, sand had begun to destroy the island of Llanddwyn and both church and well gradually became engulfed. Lewis Morris, the eighteenth-century Anglesey scholar and antiquarian, merely mentions Dwynwen's cult in passing as being of some historical interest.[60] Yet the properties of Dwynwen's Well seem to have been partly transferred to a neighbouring well dedicated to St Eilian. John Ceiriog Hughes, the popular nineteenth-century lyricist, claimed to have visited the well to seek a cure for his broken heart, but in vain. In translation his poem reads:

> I visited Llanddwynwen on a summer's day, down-hearted and lovesick. I drank of the well, but immediately turned to love my sweetheart more than ever . . . With due respect to Llanddwynwen and its foolish well, let every young man remember that no medicine, no invention, no gift, can cure the old disease of the heart completely.[61]

Lovers, it seems, were still willing to make pilgrimages to consult Dwynwen's well (or *Crochan Llanddwyn*) even at the beginning of the twentieth century, for they believed that if its waters boiled or bubbled while they performed their ceremonies it was a sign that their love would be reciprocated.[62]

During the last twenty years or so, too, as a reflection of the wider awakening of national consciousness, concerted efforts have been made to revive the festival of St Dwynwen and her status as Wales's true patron saint of lovers. Although no cards or greetings were associated with the cult originally, Dwynwen cards were produced and printed. They varied from the tasteful to the *ysmala*, comic and the *salw*, ugly or even rude variety. This, in turn, stimulated further interest in Dwynwen's feast day and it is celebrated in many parts of Wales today with discos, concerts, romantic dinners and the sending of *llateion serch,* love messengers. Yet the whole concept of this revival would seem, at present, to be rather too contrived and too commercially biased to constitute the birth or rebirth of a 'modern' Welsh folk custom.

NOTES

[1] *GDG*, 114.
[2] Ibid., 117.
[3] Ifor Williams a Thomas Roberts, (edit.) *Cywyddau Dafydd ap Gwilym a'i Gyfoeswyr,* (Cardiff, 1935), 26.
[4] *Cyfaill yr Aelwyd a'r Frythones*, 1894, p.82.
[5] *Y Brython*, 1859, p.203.
[6] D. Johnston, Canu Maswedd yr Oesoedd Canol . . . p.12.
[7] *Y Brython*, 1860, p.345.
[8] Hafod Elwy Mss 73, Robin Gwyndaf W.F.M.
[9] A Bailey Williams, p.119.
[10] Trefor M Owen, 'Hen Lythyr Caru o Lyn', *Transactions of the Caernarvonshire Historical Society*, 1959, vol.xx, pp.105-7.
[11] Stevens, pp.14-15.
[12] Stevens, photocopy of postcard.
[13] Stevens, postcard collection.
[14] W.F.M. 74.109/200.
[15] W.F.M. 64.231/20.
[16] Postcard collection of Miss Gwyneth Evans, Goitan Farm, St Nicholas, Wdig, Dyfed.
[17] *W.F.C.*, p.151.
[18] Macfarlane, p.198.
[19] H Bourne, *Antiquitates Vulgares,* (1725), Chapter 20.
[20] Hugh Hughes (edit.), p.49.
[21] *Beirdd y Berwyn,* (1902), p.78., *W.F.C.*, p.152.
[22] Dafydd Jones o Drefriw, *Blodeugerdd y Cymry,* (Holywell, 1823), p.179.
[23] *Eos Ceiriog, sef Casgliad o Ber Ganiadau Huw Morus,* (Wrexham, 1823), p.121.
[24] Gwilim Howel: *Almanaciau*, 1767-75, 3 Valentines; William Roberts, *Crefydd yr Oesoedd Tywyll*, (Carmarthen, 1852), p.62.
[25] Ruth Webb Lee, *A History of Valentines*, (1953), p.7.
[26] *W.F.C.*, p.153.
[27] Ibid., p.208; W.F.M. 28.360/1.
[28] *W.F.C.,* pp.208-9.
[29] Trefor M Owen, 'Three Merioneth Valentines', *Transactions of the Merionethshire Historical Society*, 1961-4, vol.iv, pp.72-4.
[30] *Bye-gones*, 26/12/1894.
[31] W J Davies, p.255.
[32] Ibid., p.253.
[33] Ibid., pp.253-5.
[34] I Foulkes, *Gwaith Barddonol Trefor Mai*, (Liverpool, 1883), pp.164, 315-6.
[35] D R and Z S Cledlyn Davies, *Hanes Plwyf Llanwenog*, (1939), p.117.
[36] W.F.M. Mss3472/3, p.6. Mary Jones, Pennant.
[37] W.F.M. Mss 1737/7, 46, J Ffos Davies Collection.
[38] Lee, p.76.
[39] W.F.M. Mss 3472/3, p.6.
[40] Cledlyn Davies, pp. 116-7.
[41] W.F.M. Mss 3472/3, p.6.
[42] W.F.M. 14.159/271.
[43] Ruth Webb Lee, *A History of Valentines*, (1953).
[44] *W.F.C.*, p.157.
[45] Sikes, p.259.
[46] Cledlyn Davies, p.117.
[47] *The Dewsland and Kemes Guardian,* 26/2/1881.

[48]John Jones (Myrddin Fardd), p.245.
[49]*W.F.C.*, p.155.
[50]Trevelyan, pp.244-5.
[51]S Baring-Gould and J Fisher, *Lives of the British Saints*, (London, 1908), vol.2, pp.387-392.
[52]Trevelyan, pp.243-4.
[53]*An Inventory of the Ancient Monuments in Anglesey,* The Royal Commission of Ancient and Historical Monuments.in Wales and Monmouthshire, 1937, p.119.
[54]*GDG*, 94.
[55]*O.B.W.V.*, 64.
[56]Baring-Gould, p.389.
[57]Glanmor Williams, *The Welsh Church from Conquest to Reformation,* (Cardiff, 1962), p.319.
[58]*Y Bywgraffiadur Cymreig*, (Llundain, 1953), p.505.
[59]Baring-Gould, p.389.
[60]Peter Roberts, *Yr Hynafion Cymreig*, (Carmarthen, 1823), p.174.
[61]Isaac Foulkes, *Cymru Fu*, (Wrexam, 1872), pp.423-4.
[62]Baring-Gould, p.391.

INDEX